ASPIRING TO MASTERY
The Foundation

The Secret Laws of attracting Mastery into your life.

JACQUELINE DAY

BALBOA.
PRESS

A DIVISION OF HAY HOUSE

Balboa Press books may be ordered through booksellers or by contacting:

Balboa Press
A Division of Hay House
1663 Liberty Drive
Bloomington, IN 47403
www.balboapress.com
1-(877) 407-4847

ISBN: 978-1-4525-2973-8 (sc)
ISBN: 978-1-4525-2974-5 (e)
ISBN: 978-1-4525-2975-2 (hc)

Library of Congress Control Number: 2010919005

Printed in the United States of America

Balboa Press rev. date: 1/12/2011

CONTENTS

PREFACE

In my career I have helped many people to develop their potential by using their own unique abilities and qualities. Usually people have similar things in common, to excel at their goals, to find their true destiny, develop better relationships, relieve emotional stress, increase and master their wealth, to have health and vitality, to contribute and give to their community or special charity. In other words to lead a better, fulfilled and improved life where all their needs are met.

Why do you think it is that some people seem to achieve all that they desire seemingly with little effort and with elegance while others despite all their good intentions and attempts seem to take longer to achieve their desires or even just do not ever achieve the life they are meant to be leading?

To achieve whatever it is that you choose to master or achieve in life there are certain natural laws of the universe you need to work with. It is when you work with these laws that you will attract what you want into your life. The movie the Secret enhances our awareness of The Law of Attraction. The Law of Attraction takes precedence over every other law.

In this book and program Aspiring to Mastery I have put together some very fundamental Life Principles to use along with the Law of Attraction and universal laws. I have developed this program using an A-Z of mastery. This is the foundation to master all that you wish for in your life.

Mastering these Life Principles will change your life for the better. The work book will help you to implement and perfect and apply each and every single Life Principle. Apply these Life principles to your personal life, your professional life, your relationships, your health and vitality, your wealth development, your spirituality.

Through this program you will:

- Develop your self awareness
- Develop unlimited resourcefulness
- Communicate with elegance
- Create the future you desire
- Maximise your potential
- Discover your life purpose
- Increase your belief and confidence
- Follow your bliss, radiate joy
- Be the cause of some great effects in your life
- Become focused on your goals
- Become unstoppable, achieve all that you want
- Improve your state, live with passion
- Be creative and imaginable
- Control your own happiness, health, wealth and destiny

The use of thought through the conscious mind, the unconscious mind and the universal mind are key in mastering and achieving your goals and life purpose. All these Life Principles and laws belong together, they compliment one another. You will naturally want to use each and every one of them. On completion of this life changing program, you will have a thorough understanding of mastery and how each one of these elements and principles will work to bring the results that you want in your life. Your thoughts, feelings and behaviours will attract all that you want in your life. This program offers you a step by step process to show you how you can aspire to mastery.

CHAPTER ONE

WELCOME AND INTRODUCTION

Hello and Welcome to Aspiring to Mastery. My name is Jacqueline Day and it gives me great pleasure to welcome you to this very special program that I have put together especially for you. **Aspiring to Mastery** has been a labour of love and passion for me and I look forward to you and I embarking on a wonderful journey together which will enrich your life and unlock your hidden potential.

In my work as a Master Neuro Linguistic Programmer, Master Coach, Trainer, Emotional Freedom Therapist and Inspirational Speaker, it never ceases to amaze me just how much unlimited potential we as human beings have.

The practices outlined In Aspiring to Mastery will help you to enhance and develop your self-awareness and communication which is vital in order to help you achieve your full potential. I truly believe that these practices act as a catalyst for change, maximising the potential of individuals, empowering them to reach their life successes and goals. Each and every one of these life principles in this program are the very foundation for whatever it is that you wish to master in any area of your life. Apply these principles to your business life, your relationships, your personal development, your spirituality, your physical health, your wealth development. These life principles when learnt and applied daily without fail are at the very core of mastering, manifesting and attracting what you desire in every aspect of your life. You will also notice in this program how all of these life principles and practices belong together, they are all part of a team, they all inter relate to one another, they all connect. The key is to use all of them all the time, every single day of your life; do not leave any one of them out as they will all serve you well.

In my work it is interesting to find that each individual has their own 'map of the world' and lives in a different reality from every other individual. This means that each one of us operates on our own experience of the world. I know that you may have heard the saying **'the map is not the territory'** which is a metaphor that is at the very heart of NLP. Perhaps a relevant way to express this is in the same way that a menu is not a meal , so the experience we have of the world is not the world itself. One person's perception will vary from another person's perception and their reality.

We give each event meaning and different people will give the same event a different meaning. The reason for this is that as human beings we process information through our five senses and through our brain and nervous system.

The five senses are sight, hearing, touch, smell and taste. Our mind and body connect through the nervous system and the five senses are our mental pathways that run across our body and mind. We consciously and unconsciously delete what we do not want to pay attention to. The remaining data we filter based upon our past experiences, values and beliefs. Some of the information is generalised or even distorted, some is deleted and the remainder is filtered and forms our internal map which in turn will influence our physiology and state of being.

Just like you and I are able to store and upgrade software on our Personal Computers, we can install and upgrade our mental software therefore changing the way in which we think and the actions we carry out. This has a chain reaction of sorts, since changing our thoughts will change our feelings which will in turn change our behaviour. When we change the qualities of the images, our experiences alter and it is then that new programming will take place.

New ways of thinking and solving problems can be created so that you can be at your best more often and communicate with excellence. It is important also to understand in this program that the conscious mind will hold approximately only seven pieces of information at any one time, it has the ability to accept or reject any such information.

The important difference to take on board between the conscious mind and the subconscious mind is that the sub conscious mind is more powerful and can take in hundreds and thousands of pieces of information; however it does not have the ability to accept or reject. It stores exactly what you have asked it to store from your conscious mind. It will support ALL your beliefs whether they are negative or positive. Your subconscious mind will want to prove you right and will be very loyal and obedient always thinking that it is acting in your best interest. I think that you will agree that it is important to hold our beliefs as positively as possible as they have such a powerful influence on our subconscious mind.

Our subconscious mind is perhaps the most faithful servant that we will ever have. Whatever you believe to be true your subconscious mind will strive to prove you right and fulfill your commands. If you constantly tell your subconscious mind that you are wealthy, it will move heaven and earth to manifest that reality for you encouraging you to take relevant actions. If on the other hand you are in-congruent in what you say and do and have a consciousness of lack, it will exert the same amount of force and power to manifest that reality for you. For instance if you ask for a red sports Mercedes and then you say to yourself that you will not be able to afford the running costs, you will send out confusing messages and the Mercedes will not be delivered to you. Ask, BELIEVE and receive. The secret is to really really BELIEVE. The moment you have a counter intention you do not believe it to be possible so you will not receive.

When I am working with my clients, I always provide them with a set of tools and techniques to help them develop an attitude and mindset which is outcome focussed. Their new patterns of thinking and communicating mean that their outcomes become meaningful, verifiable, compelling and achievable. They become really clear about the benefits of their goal achievement and the possible consequences if they do not start taking action soon. Much work and progress is made on exactly what was holding them back and stopping them from performing at their full potential. When I coach it is my heartiest desire that my clients are successful and develop their unlimited potential to unleash all the power that is truly within them.

Yes we really do have unlimited potential. With unlimited potential comes unlimited resourcefulness, unlimited energy, unlimited life and in life itself there is growth.

Life is not still or static, it is always moving forward and meeting forever changing conditions.

Along your life path, you may meet with many obstacles and even fears to conquer. When any fear or self doubt is resolved and released, we as human beings can move forward in ways we may not have ever imagined. What once was perceived to be an obstacle will become a challenge from which you can develop and learn from?

Now I know that you perhaps are thinking to yourself 'so Jacky what is mastery'. In this program the A-Z of Aspiring to Mastery I will explain and take you by the hand and show you many steps to aspire to the mastery that you so deserve in your life. I ask that you keep an open mind as I may well introduce you to concepts and methodologies which you have not come across before, or if you have, you may not have attempted to use them or realised the importance and power of their use.

This will be a step by step process which I will take you through with exercises for you to carry out; though I highly recommend that you read this book two or even three times before you carry out the exercises in your work book. Like so many good learning programs it is good to read the chapters several times and really absorb the information. It is when you have taken some of the meanings and concepts on board that you will be ready to explore further and carry out the exercises.

Each and every single concept that will be covered in this book has an accompanying exercise in your workbooks; some exercises may require you to pen down new thoughts and ideas, while others will suggest action items for you to include in your daily regime. Still others may outline a step or process to inculcate a particular habit into your life.

Now I know by the very fact that you have purchased this program that you are already ready to explore, to grow, to become clear about your own potential and move forward in the ways that you were meant to.

Indeed you most definitely can be the master of your own destiny and the star of your own show.

There are some very important and fundamental processes and laws for you to follow which will enable you to create the future that you so desire. Have you ever been at a crossroads in your life? I am sure that you can relate to that feeling. The choices that you are making at this very moment are designing your own future. Do you ever wonder or ponder on what might have been? What would have happened if you had made a different choice or made a different decision? I am sure you must have. I know that I can relate to this.

It is here that I would like to share with you a story, one of which I have not shared with many, only because I suppose it happened some time ago. In fact, I am about to take you back to my early school days. And yes this IS a very relevant story. At the age of eleven I was chosen and put forward to sit for the Art Exam to enable me to enter the only Art School in England for eleven to eighteen year olds.

One could not apply to sit this exam; you were actually chosen to sit it. I remember the halls of my junior school were full of my art work. Art was a passion for me, one of my biggest thrills. My Head Mistress and Form teacher entered me for this very unique school. I was thrilled when

I passed and entered into a school which I loved, doing something that I loved. Every day I looked forward with great joy to going to school. Now I remember very clearly that there were two boys in my form whose art work I admired greatly and in ' my world' they had mastered every possible skill in the art world. Their paintings really did come to life. I thought my art work could not compare.

So I chose to take a different career into business. Some while later there was a school reunion which I attended with ex-pupils from all the years. As I met with one of the boys in my class whose work I had so admired, it was wonderful to hear of his progress in the Art world and even to the extent that Andrew Lloyd Webber, the master of Theatre, had bought some of his paintings. I was fascinated and pleased for him. I also met with a girl from my form that made the following statement to me "Jacky, I remember you for three things". Intrigued, I asked what they were. Her reply was. "Your wonderful mane of long red hair; your ability to find fun and joy in everything – you giggled into every lesson and you giggled out of every lesson; most of all though, I remember you for your amazing art work". This was one of those defining moments. Yes my Art work was amazing. It was just different to others. After all an artist or master should be unique shouldn't they?

Now I wanted to tell you this story for many reasons. Let's think, what does this story tell you about me at that time in my life?

Well first of all I can definitely say that I was comparing myself to others. This was mistake number one. I here and now state to you.

Never ever compare yourself to others. The only person you need ever compare yourself with is yourself.

That is what really matters. Compare yourself to how well you are doing now and how you have progressed since yesterday, last week, last month, last year. Master your unique talents and abilities and continue to make good progress. Ensure that you take the best that you have achieved and install it within you. Focus on what does work for you and upon this build a good self representation.

What else does it tell you about me at that time? I think my own self belief was for some reason in neglect. Now why did I not believe in myself when others believed in me when I was eleven years of age; yes they recognised a talent as did my peers later on.

What was my thought process at that time?

It also tells you that I had been doing something I loved since the age of eleven and I had the ability to find and radiate joy, which is so hard for many of us to do on a daily basis.

I would also say that this story tells you that I also lacked a sound decision making strategy at that time. Yes, I was at a crossroads. A very vital crossroads - my future career. The choices and decisions I made at that time could have sent me in a completely different direction from where I am today.

Just as a leader in the science of peak performance, Anthony Robbins states "It is in your moment of decision that your destiny is shaped". This is so very true. Every decision we make shapes our destiny. The reason you are where you are right now is a result of every decision you have ever made in your life. Think about it. That thought alone is very powerful and does make us pause for a second. That thought means that you alone are responsible for where you are today based on the choices you made in the past and you alone will be responsible for where you will be tomorrow based on the choices you are making right now.

If I had had this certain knowledge at that time in my life along with the tools and resourcefulness that I possess today, I may have made very different decisions. This story of my school days is so very relevant to this program Aspiring To Mastery.

Our thoughts, feelings, actions and behaviours attract into our life exactly what we send out and transmit. It is likely that you have seen the movie The Secret and so you will have heard about the Law of Attraction. I will be referring to both The Secret and The Law of Attraction at many points along this program and together we will learn how to use this knowledge along with some techniques from NLP and other practices to achieve mastery in our lives.

In the story of my school days, I have mentioned the following concepts - belief, love, joy, passion, strategy, thought. These alone could have changed my life and indeed my destiny.

They can change your life too for the better once you have mastered them. Yet these are just a few of the subjects which we are going to cover together in this program Aspiring to Mastery.

There are many aspects of Mastery which I have felt compelled to write about and share with you and these are the most essential ingredients to help you along your path to mastery.

Whenever you find yourself at a crossroads in your life you will have all the resourcefulness of these Life Principles to enable you to make the right decisions as you have gained a clearer understanding of your own infinite potential. Like life itself you will have power in the knowledge that you will not stand still and you will continue to grow.

Just as when you first take on a new sport or exercise; your muscles become stronger in time and practice. When you learn each new tool and subject in this program and practice it, your ability to use and apply these tools will become stronger over time.

I want you to be able to draw upon these resources and use them whenever you can until they too are a built in habit which you practice every single day of your life. When they become a habit, make a note of everything that happens in your life, everything that YOU have attracted into your life. Notice what has changed in your life. Notice what changes there are within you. Notice also your successes, your achievements. Notice what you have really mastered and what you and mastery have done for one another and for those that you serve.

You will be developing your Life Principles to enable your accomplishments to stand out, yet to you they will be the habits that you have formed so will seemingly be quite normal. This force will work with you and fears and failures will become non-existent as a new confidence and other positive transformations take place. A new power will surface as your mind masters these principles. That is the power to be what you WILL to be.

You may be wondering if all this is possible. Abandon such thoughts right at this minute for these are the very thoughts which are stopping you from moving forward. Once more, I recall, again from my school days a short anecdote to tell you.

When I was young my most favourite Shakespeare play was Twelfth Night. One of the famous quotes in this play was "Some are born great, some achieve greatness, others have greatness thrust upon them".

In this program Aspiring to Mastery you and I shall be looking at those who achieve greatness and mastery in their life and how this is also within your reach. There were times gone by when the Aristocracy thought it to be sacrilegious to rise above the position you were born to in life. Any thought of advancing yourself had to be abandoned. Thank goodness this is no longer the case. In the modern world individuals need not accept the world that they were born to. The will and the desire for self improvement has produced much progress in ways that were once unimaginable. The evidence is all around us. Communication and travel and other great inventions are the result of those who began from humble beginnings and through discipline, will, belief and inner force achieved success from which many of us benefit.

Many if not all of the ingredients and principles of mastery are within you right now. The secret is to know how to access them, open the door to them, understand them and learn how they work and then practice the use of them until it becomes second nature to you. Like a powerful gale, the power is within you waiting to be unleashed.

This program I have designed for you will result in teaching you how to unleash this internal power providing you practice, practice and yes you have guessed it PRACTISED some more. Like many great professionals will tell you, once you have mastered the art of practice - you CANNOT GET IT WRONG. The application of these principles is a law unto itself.

Now it is important to realise that your thoughts enable you to control your very own happiness, health, fortune and destiny. For when you master the quality of your thoughts you will find within you a power so strong that indeed you WILL to attract all that you need to manifest all the qualities that your thoughts determine.

Now there are times for instance, and I know that you will relate to this, for some reason we have forgotten a person's name or cannot quite remember a certain fact or date. I know this happens to me sometimes. Instead of telling myself that no matter what I just cannot remember, for I know that this is not true, I silently say to myself 'I am searching for this right now' or 'please recollect this for me'. This command is heard by my inner conscious and very soon after the correct information just comes to me without endless mental exertion. My outer conscious can now access the information quite comfortably.

For our sub conscious mind is quite certainly a storehouse, and just as you store items in your cupboards and storage rooms and at times have to search for them, you have stored much knowledge into your sub conscious mind though it may not be a systematic storing of information. With the correct use of thought the search becomes much easier.

Also I add to demonstrate this, there are times when I have to travel some distance with my work and that can entail waking up earlier than my normal time for I may have an early train to catch or may need to be at the airport by a certain time, or often I have appointments at certain times. The messages that I have relayed to my subconscious mind will never let me down. I naturally awake on time before my physical alarm clock goes off so that I catch that early train or plane, I naturally look at my watch before the appointment due time. This is my mental alarm clock working for it has been embedded into my sub conscious mind by the messages I have relayed to it from my conscious mind.

When I first became inspired and compelled to write this program for you Aspiring to Mastery, I knew that it would be the latter part of the year before I would have the time to sit down and write an in-depth program due to my otherwise busy schedule. However, the idea and passion for this program came to me at least twelve months prior to me actually sitting down to develop the program.

In the interim period I visualised this quite strongly and clearly. I had a passionate desire to help you on your path to Mastery. I placed it in my vision book; I meditated on it; I visualised it; I made notes whenever an idea came to me so that I had began to actually work on it; I gave my goal a completion date; I aligned the goal with other projects that I had. All my observations, creativity, passion, vision, thoughts, desire, ambitions were passed into my subconscious. All the time my subconscious mind was recognising, collating, storing, organising, making connections, digesting.

I was safe and confident in the knowledge that nothing would ever be lost and I could not possibly forget anything that I had placed in the store cupboard of my mind. I knew my dream would become a reality. All my answers were within. And you can do the same with just about anything that you wish to master in your life. A technique I also used throughout the twelve months is one in which I have used and taught many times in the workshops I have tutored in. That is the Walt Disney Planning Strategy. Walt Disney, who is perhaps one of the most inspirational men and geniuses of our time, had his Dream Room, his Planning Room and his Critically Analysing Room. Just like Walt Disney, I would analyse and criticise the plan and make adjustments going backwards and forwards from Planning to Critically Analysing. Just like Walt Disney I never ever criticised the Dream. My Dream had to stay intact. It had to stay as positive as the bliss and the goal I was following. I would never criticise my dream.

I am now delivering and sharing that dream with you. I truly and sincerely wish that after you have completed this special life changing program on Aspiring to Mastery that you too will share your dreams and the results you have manifested in your life with me. I invite you to let me know how this program has transformed your life and I look forward to celebrating your success and achievements with you.

Now this leads me to sharing with you how the world within you is a mirror reflection of the world without. This is shown in our sorrows, disappointments, sufferings, tears, joy, laughter, pleasure, happiness. This is a result of the effect that something has had upon us. Now when we have these experiences in life - do we stop and really reflect upon what has caused this and just where that cause came from. What exactly is this cause and effect in which so much is spoken of.

After all, we can do all that we think we are doing in order to prevent a disaster in our life, yet still for instance after all the saving, planning and safety measures we made our investments and equity may fall into decline; the weather may be bad making travel difficult so we decide to stay at home to avoid an accident yet we slip on the ice in our own garden and have an injury. Do you think for a moment that the thought of avoiding an accident meant that as this is what you were focusing on, the impression made upon your subconscious mind was 'accident' or 'disaster' and that is exactly what you received? Do you think this may have been the cause? Do you think that you may have without intention, invited this to happen?

Remember that though your subconscious mind is unbelievably powerful, it will not register the word 'don't; so for your subconscious mind – slip on the ice, and don't slip on the ice, mean the same thing, because it simply will not process the word 'don't', in both cases the faithful servant that is your subconscious mind will ensure that you do indeed – slip on the ice. For this was your command.

As I write this, the weather in England over this festive season is cold, icy, snowing, foggy, and with sub-zero and minus temperatures. Travel conditions have not been good all across the nation. Not once did I think I will not travel as I may have an accident. Perish such thoughts. The truth is, and I will now let you into a secret. Before the snow arrived I had already made up my mind not to travel the long distance that I usually travel during the festive period. I had already decided to focus on this special program I am writing for you - Aspiring to Mastery - as I wanted to make good progress with it and ensure that I met the goals that I had set myself.

When the snow did arrive, not once did I think it was a good job I was not travelling long distance as I may have had an accident. Instead I totally focused on my goal and on being cosy and warm and inspired to continue with my plan. I still had a great festive time attending festive services, doing voluntary work for people in need, eating and sharing moments with friends and going on long beach walks which I love. New Years day I had the opportunity to spend time with my friends and we walked for three hours on the beach where despite the temperatures the sun was shining and shimmering on the ocean. It was perfect. On New Year's Eve too I was greatly moved and inspired by the blue moon which you may have noticed and this is the first time in many years that this phenomenon has occurred on New Year's Eve. It was awe inspiring and quite magical. I did not slip on the ice in my garden and I did not have an injury! I focused on the beauty, joy and the magic the universe has to offer and followed my bliss in writing this program.

My cause has created some great effects and yours can do the same by following the laws that this program on Aspiring to Mastery has to teach you. **Remember that the conditions and the results are the effects and that thoughts are the causes.** This lesson alone is so powerful and will help you to manifest more of what you actually DO WANT in your life. Understanding this will bring you a great sense of freedom, more than you could ever imagine. The true masters in life always think of ways in which they can succeed. Failure is not an option to them. Success is their only thought. In the words of Shakespeare "There is nothing either good or bad, but thinking makes it so". As we all know Shakespeare produced pages after pages of great work and was a true Master in every sense of the word. When good is the cause, then the effect will also be good.

In this program Aspiring to Mastery we will be talking further on the power of thought. For when we truly understand that there is only thought and the power of the mind is eternal and supreme, then becomes the realisation of Universal Mind which we shall also talk more of in this program.

This will disperse all fears and doubts which in itself is transforming. Having no fear means fearing nothing, dreading nothing and stopping at nothing and having the faith and courage to become unstoppable, overcome adversity and become unconquerable.

What an unlimited human being you will become with unlimited potential. You will be truly amazing. Yet the biggest realisation of all is that wealth too is thought. Yes wealth is thought! Riches and wealth start with an idea which starts in the mind. This realisation I know for me was a major turning point in my life. Just think about it. Think of all the great inventions in life, they all began with an idea, they began with a thought. And does that not mean that as thought is also within you that wealth and riches are ALSO within YOU. Your rich life is within you. Developing your ideas now may well be the outlet that attracts wealth to you.

The secret is to perfect this and to find the need and the way in which you can be of service and supply that need. It is here though that mediocrity may well be a sin. You will need to stand tall, provide extra value, and make more effort with extraordinary results. Remember here also the law of compensation, that of cause and effect which we have already mentioned. Usually we receive in greater proportion to that which we give out. Become an unlimited human being.

You and I are the apprentices of the world as indeed we all are. Great masters demonstrate their thirst and yearning for learning. They are ferocious readers. This is a trait which all masters have and one in which you will emulate on your journey to mastery. Masters are coachable and teachable and open to learning. What is your willingness to learn? What priority is it in your life; what sacrifices will you make in order to learn; what are you willing to give up? What time, effort and money will you commit in order to learn? In order to get different results in your life, I am sure that you will agree that you will need to do something different. This means that if you want things in your life to change, changes must be made in your life. Your continuous education and learning are vital ingredients of mastery. All masters experience that when their desire increases so does their willingness to learn increase. Observing mentors is a way to accelerate your learning.

When you take 100% responsibility for everything that happens in your life you become of the realisation that you created it. You and only you have created what is in your life so does it not then make sense to realise that if you created it so too you can change it. Taking complete responsibility releases you from being a victim. You then step into your very own empowerment. Reducing all doubt will increase your belief. To reduce doubt your positive energy will need to be stronger than your negative energy. Your positive energy must be predominant, imagine it as a giant ball which gathers up more and more positive energy. Consciously transmit your thoughts into strong desires of everything you want in your life. Become strongly emotionally involved with all that you desire. Attach strong positive emotions to your desires.

Know that you get what you think about most of the time. Thoughts are physical and go out to the universe. When defining your dream be specific and define just how good you will feel. Act as though you already have achieved your dream and goal along with the emotions you have for it. Feel good. Make feeling good your goal. Do not be blinkered.

Many people block their potential. They do not see how they can possibly achieve. They look within their radar only. Step outside your radar. Everything that is yours is outside of your radar. Looking outside your radar will make shifts in your life. It is then that everything moves. Life is not still or static. Life has to move. Make those shifts in your life now. Look outside your radar. Raise your vibrational energies. Transmit higher vibrations to the universe. What does feeling good mean to you? Define your feel good emotions – be outrageously happy, extra confident, exhilarated, blessed, grateful, appreciative, excited, and loving. Feel good NOW. Why delay feeling good? You can feel this way now. Think happy positive thoughts. Your mind is a frequency of information. The vibration of your frequency is like a magnet and like will be drawn to you. Ask yourself what wonderful amazing things will happen to you today. Expect wonderful and amazing things to happen. Everything is energy, a vibration. Put out the frequencies of what you want. Do this daily. Do not miss a day. This is living the law of attraction which supersedes all other laws. Have that burning desire, transmit the energy constantly and daily, have absolute belief, have no doubt and take the actions to increase the vibration to attract all that you want to BE, DO and HAVE in your life.

Every morning and night ask yourself what you are thankful for, grateful for, what were your successes? Let the answers unfold and write them down. When you get the results that you want in life they should not be a surprise to you if you have been living in positive expectation. Belief without doubt is positive expectation. You will naturally love what you are doing and actions will also become a joy to you. You will want to take action. Develop positive predominant thought patterns. Work on your positive emotions to feel good all the time. When anything happens in your life that you were not expecting such as losing your job, your vibrations still need to be positive. See such matters as a blessing. Acknowledge the situation and if at the time you do not see the reason simply say to yourself, "I cannot see the reason for this right now, however I know that this will turn out to my advantage for my needs were not being met and I can now focus on and create what I really do want in my life." pop the champagne and celebrate for life is giving you an opportunity to shift! Say to yourself "everything will work out well". Work through the situation and move on with positive expectation. Create your chief aim for your future. Become obsessed with what you want. Let mastery become your driver.

CHAPTER TWO

OVERVIEW OF A-Z OF MASTERY

This program is like a great adventure for the two of us. Let us together recap on your introduction to this program in chapter one where we covered so much ground, though just the tip of the fountain of joy which we shall embrace throughout this program. In chapter one you and I were introduced to one another. Unlimited potential and some of the aspects of mastery were covered along with the positive impact they will have on your life and how they will change your life for the better. The meaning of cause and effect was briefly discussed. The way in which the conscious mind and the subconscious mind operate the power of our thoughts and the messages which we transmit to the Universe were quite astounding revelations.

I'd like to talk now about what is mastery and why it is important for us to aspire to achieve it. The opposite of mastery is mediocrity and that can lead to failure. When we are living our lives in either of these two states of mediocrity and failure it will lead to feelings of unhappiness, discontent, and other unpleasant experiences.

It is only when we decide to excel at something or when we decide to aspire to mastery that our life becomes full of passion and purpose and excitement.

Mastery is the decision to excel at something and the desire to make or contribute something positive and worthwhile to the world. Some examples of individuals who have attained mastery in their lives are, Tiger Woods as a great golfer, Brian Tracy as the master of influence and personal development, Anthony Robbins as the greatest self-help coach the world has ever known.

I will be most honest with you, the road to mastery is a labour in itself and it is paved with challenges, however the rewards are well worth it. You may ask then, why do so few people aspire to mastery? It is much like the story I told you earlier about my childhood and my own self-beliefs, very few people believe they have the potential to aspire to mastery. The very fact that you have purchased this program and are reading this book, tells me that you are one of these special few people who believe in their own potential and capacity to achieve mastery.

As I have mentioned before this is a wonderful comprehensive program. It has an extremely detailed book, which I have broken up into bite size chapters. It also comes with an accompanying workbook to help you implement and apply each of the concepts that we will be talking about in the book. I do recommend that you take the time to listen to read each chapter two to three times BEFORE you pick up your workbooks, this will help you understand each concept in detail and will also pre-pare you to complete the exercise which will inculcate that concept into your life.

Throughout the program I will also be referring to quotes from many famous people, along with many tips and techniques for you to incor-porate into your life. This is a journey that we will undertake together. Think of me as your guide, illuminating your way along this wonderful path; together we will learn more about each other and about the world around us. Together we will aspire to mastery and together we will find ways to help us attain it.

You will find that each chapter in this program has a purpose and is structured in a particular way to make for easy comprehension. In chapter 1, I introduced myself to you and then I talk about the purpose of this program, about myself, about mastery and about the things that you can expect to learn from this program.

In chapter 3 – chapter 7 we will talk about the various concepts that make up this program – Aspiring to Mastery, and in chapter 8, we will review each concept in brief along with the progress that you would have made in your workbooks.

Let's talk now about what exactly you are going to learn in this program, shall we?

This program the A-Z of Aspiring to Mastery, is a series of steps which I have structured using the letters of the alphabet from A to Z. Given the nature of the program however and the variety of concepts covered you may find that each letter can have up to 5 different subjects being discussed under it, some may have one or two, but most have more than that. Each of these concepts is then accompanied by an exercise or discussion in your A-Z of Mastery Workbooks.

We begin by talking about the importance of ACTION and the consequences of not taking action at the right time. We also spend some time discussing the examples of famous individuals like Walt Disney and Mahatma Gandhi. We end by talking about the two kinds of action that exist – mental action and physical action.

You will also learn about the power of BELIEF, why belief is such an important factor in attaining mastery, what are the things we should believe in, including how to believe in ourselves, in the people around us and most importantly in the Universe that we live in.

The three C's of COURAGE, CONFIDENCE and COMMITMENT will help you to find the courage to live your dreams and to pursue them with vigour and intensity. Confidence is also a trait shared by masters around the world and across many fields. Together we will discover why confidence is important, where does confidence come from, and how to improve our confidence. Lastly, we will also talk about commitment and the importance of being committed to our goal of aspiring to mastery.

The letter D stands for one sole word with a lot of weight attached to it – DICIPLINE. We will discuss why it is important for us to have discipline in our lives. Also we will learn about the theory of motivation and the 4 stages of motivation and the differences between internal and external motivation. As with each concept there is an exercise included to help you become more disciplined about your life and achieving your goals.

Then we move on to the subject of life-long continuous EDUCATION. You will learn what a WIIFM or a What's In It for Me is, and how to find your WIIFM to learn. We will also discuss the different ways we can continue our education, both formally and informally, and also devise an action plan to enable us to incorporate the habit of learning into our daily lives. Also the importance of learning from other masters already qualified in your subject. I can truly state how important this has been on my journey of personal development. I have been very honoured to have the experience of training with Bob Proctor who has many years experience of working in the area of mind potential and who also featured in the blockbuster movie the Secret. For my NLP Master Practitioner I qualified with the co-creator of NLP Richard Bandler. I also learnt from John LaValle who has trained people in fortune 100 companies for more than 15 years and also teaches with Richard Bandler. I have the privilage of Teaching the philosophies of Louise L Hay. I have taken the opportunity to attend seminars and learnings with some of the world top personal development coaches such as Anthony Robbins and Brian Tracy. Education is truly continuous for we never stop learning. Continuous education is essential for mastery.

Now the next part of mastery I want to share with you is F which stands for FOREGIVENESS, FOCUS and FAITH. In this section we will learn how to forgive, really and truly forgive, this means people around as and most importantly ourselves. We will also learn how to cultivate a habit which is truly wonderful to have, the habit of focus. It is important to remember that **what we focus on expands;** so what do you want to expand in your life? We take examples from self-development leaders like Brian Tracy and Anthony Robbins in how to develop focus. Finally we will discuss the subject of Faith and how faith in your abilities, in your goals and in your beliefs is the key to achieving mastery in your life.

Together you and I will now look at how to master GOALS and GRATITUDE. We will talk about the difference between goals and dreams. Also we will discuss the importance of Goal setting in mastery, and why a well written goal is more powerful than a spoken goal or thinking about it. Together we will talk about the benefits of goal setting and also detail the goal setting process; lastly we will discover the correct way to frame a goal when writing it using the 6 P's of positive, personal, present, possible, performance related and pen it down.

Our next discussion on mastery is that of Gratitude, and why gratitude is one of the well kept secrets of the law of attraction and also perhaps the most powerful one. We will find out together why gratitude must become a way of life for us. I will also share with you some of my favourite ways to harness the power of gratitude in your life.

The 3 H's are the HOLISTIC APPROACH, HEALTH and HARMONY. The Holistic approach is the most successful approach to treating many difficult and often fatal conditions; it is also a fabulous way to achieve mastery by focussing on wellness in all aspects of your life, mind, emotion and spirit.

Harmony is another key concept. In this program and through it we learn the concept of balance in all aspects of our life. We will discover how to achieve harmony both within and without, and also harmony between what we say, what we think, what we feel and what we do. Examine if you are in harmony in all aspects of your life, such as career, financial, relationships, personal development, spirituality.

The 4 I's stand for INSPIRATION, INNOVATION, INVINCIBLE and IMAGINATION. We will discuss what exactly constitutes innovation in this part of the program, and how inspiration is different from motivation. I will also provide you with my top 8 tips to help you get inspired during those times when you find it hard to channel your inner genius.

We will also discuss the meaning of being invincible, and how to be invincible we need to first seek self-knowledge. We must also love ourselves and build up the courage to stand for what we believe in. Innovation is yet another key to mastery in this program, and here we will talk about what innovation is and how it is different from invention. We will also discuss ways to become more innovative. The last I stands for imagination and in this portion of the book we will discuss why imagination is vital to us when aspiring to mastery. We will also explore the benefits of imagination, and how to develop our ability in this area.

No program on mastery would be complete without a discussion on JOY and here you will learn about what being joyful means, why it is beneficial to be joyful, and how you can learn to cultivate joy in your life. If you have watched the movie – The Secret, you will remember a line from the movie – "follow your bliss", here we will talk about what exactly it means to follow your bliss, and how you can follow your bliss.

It is also a true fact that one of the steps to personal mastery is learning how to be kind. In this program I will show you how to be kind first and foremost to yourself, for only when we learn KINDNESS towards ourselves, can we be kind towards others. We will then talk about ways to be kind to ourselves on a daily basis, and then move on to discussing how to be kind to the people around us.

KARMA is a concept that comes to us from ancient Hinduism, in this program we will talk about the concept of karma – the law of cause and effect and the consequence of our actions both in this life and the next. The law of Karma can have a profound effect on how we live our lives especially as aspiring masters.

We then move on to LEVERAGE and LOVE. By leverage we mean the ability to attain maximum output with minimum input. In leverage we will talk about our strengths and how to make the most of them to help us achieve mastery. We also explore how to leverage other people in order to achieve our goals and our dreams. Finally we will talk about the use of tools to achieve our goals.

It has been said that love makes the world go round, and our program on Aspiring to Mastery would certainly not be complete without a discussion on the subject of love and how love can help us attain our goals of mastery. Though we will not discuss every aspect of love in our program we will definitely discuss why love is such an important aspect of achieving mastery. We will also talk about how the decision to bring love into your life is a conscious choice, and not a chance act. Loving yourself is perhaps the most important love affair you will have in your life and we discuss how we need to learn to fall in love with ourselves and people in general. Finally I will talk to you about the importance of loving what you do and doing what you love.

By now I am sure you have a fair idea of the concepts and the ideas that you can look forward to learning about, and you also have a good understanding of the program format and what this program entails.

We then discuss the 4 M's of MINDSET, MODELLING, MAGNETIC and MEDITATION. I cannot stress on the importance of a positive mental attitude or mindset, and how every single experience that we have in our lives is the result of our mindset at the time. If you take one thing and one thing only from this program on Aspiring to Mastery, let it be the importance of a positive mental mindset.

I know that this may be easier said than done which is why I will share with you some ways to help you develop a positive mental mindset, and the advantages of maintaining one.

We will also talk about the concept of modelling which is a concept borrowed from the world of psychology and NLP. Modelling means to incorporate the behaviour of people who are successful, wealthy, and accomplished into our own lives.

Have you ever wanted to have a magnetic personality like Bill Clinton, or Princess Diana? Well in this section of Aspiring to Mastery I will reveal to you exactly what it takes to develop a magnetic personality, like these famous individuals.

Almost all the masters that we will refer to and quote throughout this program have extolled the virtues and usefulness of the practice of meditation in their daily lives and as a tool to help them achieve mastery. I will help you through the process of meditation, the benefits of the practice and also help you experience meditation for the first time if you have never done it before.

I have said it before and I will say it again, to achieve mastery it takes practice and persistence. In order for us to achieve our dreams, reach our goals and to be true masters we must cultivate a never give up attitude. We will spend some time talking about what a NEVER GIVE UP Attitude is, why having one is important and how to go about cultivating such an attitude.

The attitude of OPTIMISM is an interesting one, and I will reveal to you the details of why both optimism and pessimism are self-fulfilling prophecies. Which means that if you believe in the positive more of the same will come to you and if you believe in the negative, more of the same will come to you as well?

I am also going to reveal to you the top 3 reasons why you should be an optimist and my four done and tested ways to become an optimist.

We are also special human beings, we have all been placed on this earth with our own special set of strengths and talents and uniqueness. However, many of us and this has happened to me in the past, forget to embrace our individuality and we strive to become one of the masses. There are huge rewards to be reaped from being original and like any other skill or habit in this program; it is a skill that can be learnt slowly and with time. ORIGINALITY will make you stand out from the masses.

Another interesting concept that you will come across in this chapter is that of building your belief in yourself as being OMNIPOTENT or all powerful. As you will discover when you read this portion of the book, this is another self-fulfilling prophecy that you will learn about.

If you want to achieve anything in your life and I really mean anything, you need to be passionate. True masters know that without passion they are just like everybody else. PASSION is what really and truly sets them apart.

I am sure you have heard it said that you must have passion for what you do. However I am going to go a step further and I am going to reveal to you ways to install more passion in your work and in your life. I started off this program – Aspiring To Mastery by talking about the unlimited potential that each and every one of us has. In this chapter, I am going to help you understand what holds you back from reaching your full potential, and also you will complete an exercise on achieving your potential in your A-Z of Mastery Workbook.

Many of the people we have spoken about in this program, many of the great masters that we have quoted or learnt from are also great philanthropists. Using their examples I will reveal to you why the art of PHILANTHROPY like the secret of gratitude are tools you can use to create the life that you want.

Another very interesting concept that you will learn about in this program – Aspiring to Mastery, is the ability to be QUALITATIVE, or the habit of focussing on quality versus quantity in any interaction. I will share with you ways to incorporate quality into every aspect of your daily life.

We will also talk about another trait which is common to many famous and accomplished people, the tendency to be quick witted, or quick to think and quick to act. While you may have thought that you are either born quick witted or you are not, I will prove this belief wrong and show you ways to be more QUICK WITTED from today.

The 3 R's stand for RESPONSIBILITY, RIGOUR and REASON. As the law of attraction teaches us, we are each responsible for the reality that we create. In this section we will talk about the meaning of responsibility, for ourselves, our actions and our thoughts. We will also talk about ways to take responsibility for our lives.

I will also talk to you about Rigour and what it means to be able to do something consistently over time to achieve results. Lastly we will talk about Reason, and why it is important for us to have a reason for everything that we do in our lives. A strong reason can make achieving many things in our life worthwhile.

For the letter S, we have as many as 5 concepts that we will be discussing – SOLUTIONS, STRATEGY, SYSTEMS, SPIRIT, STRENGTH and SERVICE. First, I will talk to you about how Masters focus on the solution to a problem as opposed to the cause of the problem or the problem itself.

While the word strategy is more often heard in the halls of a company head office than on a program on mastery, you will learn why it is absolutely vital for you as a person to have a personal strategy in place with clear cut objectives that you want to achieve.

I will also reveal to you an NLP technique called the TOTE model, which you can use to become more efficient at what you do. The use of efficient systems is another concept that we have borrowed from well run companies. Systems can help us on our path to mastery by creating automatic check lists and processes to simplify our lives and make us more efficient.

The word Spirit, has many different meanings. However, in this program I use it to describe a vital and animating force that comes from within you. It is the ability to live with vitality, energy, enthusiasm and confidence, and through this program I will endeavour to teach you how to do just that.

Another vital key in this program is Strength, specifically inner strength that we must all rely on when times are tough, or when we feel that we are being overcome with fear and obstacles. Our inner strength is what helps us overcome such times.

Lastly in S, I will talk about Service. We will talk about how you can be of service to others, how can you add value to their lives. Being of service to others is another key factor in achieving mastery.

Before we go on to discuss what you will learn in the rest of Aspiring To Mastery, take a moment to think and review the many learnings you have already encountered on this program. I am confident that you are enjoying your program on Aspiring to Mastery so far. Remember if you want to, you can read any portion of this program again, or as many times as you want until you are ready to move on to the next section of the program. You will get a chance to dive in and use your workbooks soon; also if you would like the audio version of this program, for easy listening, you can purchase it from where you bought the Book and Workbook.

Zig Ziglar one of my favourite motivational speakers and a top sales guru, always talks about how he used to listen to motivational tapes and books while driving from one sale to the next early on in his career. He credits this habit as one of the most important factors that helped him reach where he is in terms of mastery and success. I encourage you to be like Zig and play Aspiring to Mastery in your car when you are driving to work, or at any point in your day when you have some time and could use some inspiration and encouragement. Fill your hours with material that inspires you to attain your goals and very soon you will find yourself attaining them.

There are 3 interesting concepts which are those of TENACITY, THOUGHT and TRUTH. We will talk about how Tenacity is persistence in seeking something we value or desire. We will also discuss the virtue of being able to Think in order to achieve mastery and success. Lastly we will talk about the ability to be truthful and what it means to be true to ourselves and our values 100% of the time.

In this penultimate chapter we will also talk about the UNIVERSAL MIND and the power that we can tap into if we wish too. I will also teach you what it means to become UNSTOPPABLE and how you can become unstoppable on your quest to aspiring to mastery.

The 4 V's here stand for VALUES, VISION, VIBRATION and VITALITY. Borrowing from the principles of corporate companies we must have a vision statement which provides us with direction and guidance in our lives. In this part of the program I will walk you through the steps to enable you to write your own vision statement. We will also discuss why it is vital to be able to raise your vibration and how to raise your vibration in order to manifest the things that you want in your life.

V also stands for Vitality and we will talk about why it is important to live a life of vitality, and how to become more energetic and enthusiastic about life.

In W we will talk about WILL, a vital ingredient in helping us attain mastery. We will also explore WISDOM and how it is possible for us to become wise and make wisdom an aspect of our lives. WEALTH is something that each and every one of us aspires to. The accumulation and cultivation of wealth is a secret known by all masters. I will reveal to you the secrets of attracting wealth, and I will also reveal to you a ten step process to attracting more wealth into your life.

Now, have you heard of the X-FACTOR or that certain special uniqueness that makes some people stand out from the crowd? With this program you will learn what that X-factor is and why it is important to have it, and also ways in which to find your own X-factor.

Our last two letters stand for YEN, ZEN, ZEST and ZEAL. Yen is an unquestionable, burning desire to achieve the things that we want in life. Zen is another Japanese word that means meditation; however more than that it is a way of life which teaches focus and mastery by looking within. Zest is energy and we will learn how to be zestful and energetic, brimming with enthusiasm and vitality. The last concept that we cover in this program is Zeal or the eagerness to achieve all our goals and desires.

I know many of you are thinking there is so much to master in mastery. You do want to succeed in mastery don't you? That's right, you do. In your eagerness you will naturally want to read the next chapter so you can begin your journey of Aspiring to Mastery.

Before you do that, I would like you to turn to the first exercise in your workbooks; here you will find some questions that I would like you to answer before you move onto the next part of this program. You will need a few minutes to complete this exercise.

1. Why do I want to complete this program – Aspiring to Mastery?

2. What are my expectations from this program?

3. What do I hope to achieve by the end of this program?

4. How do I see this program helping me in my life?

5. Are there any specific goals or outcomes I want to achieve upon completion of this program?

6. What is my level of commitment to this program, what am I willing to do to achieve mastery in my life

7. What other questions or thoughts do I have about the program?

This brings us to the end of chapter two of Aspiring to Mastery. You now have a good understanding of who I am and why I am qualified to teach this course; you are aware of the program structure and the different tools that you will be using as we cover each aspect. You have read a brief description of each concept that we will be covering from A-Z in chapters 3 to 7and you have also just completed your first exercise in your workbooks. Congratulations!

CHAPTER THREE

FROM ACTION TO EDUCATION

ACTION

The first step to mastery which I want to introduce to you begins with the letter 'A' and 'A' stands for Action. To achieve mastery in any aspect of your life whether it's personal or professional you must set yourself certain goals to achieve and it is only after you have achieved these goals you will say that you have achieved mastery in your life. As many a famous person would tell us the first step to achieving any goals that we set for ourselves in life is to take action towards those goals.

I truly believe that action is the single most vital factor that separates those of us who merely dream about achieving great things and those of us who translate our dreams into reality.

Newton's laws of motion, while mostly used by physicists and scientists can be drawn on to shed some light on the importance of the principle of Action. Newton's first law of motion states that "Every body continues in its state of rest or motion unless it is acted upon by an external force". If we apply this law to our lives, we understand that our lives will continue to remain the way they are unless we ourselves exert an external force on them – in this case that force is called action.

Newton's second law states that the force applied to a body produces a proportional acceleration. If we translate this to our lives and our own mastery we can see that the greater the action, the greater is our acceleration towards our goals. Thus action is directly proportional to another word beginning with an 'A' - achievement. The bigger the action – the bigger the achievement!

Newton's third law states that every action produces an equal and op-posite reaction. In other words if you place your finger on a stone and press it, then your finger exerts pressure on the stone, and an equal and opposite pressure is exerted on your finger by the stone. If we apply this law to our lives we can see that any action that we take towards achiev-ing our goals or mastery has an equal or opposite reaction which also exerts an action on us in drawing us towards them.

Throughout history we can see examples of famous people who took action in order to achieve their dreams or their goals despite criticism, opposition and the impracticality of their dreams. Walt Disney took action to convert his dream of a magical place for people to come and spend time into Disneyland – a place that truly is a magical place for people of all ages.

Mahatma Gandhi, who was single-handedly responsible for India gain-ing freedom from the imperial rule through his non-violent and peace-ful protests, translated his belief that India should be a free nation into an action that galvanized an entire population to action and achieved freedom for millions of people.

Thomas Edison – the father of electricity took thousands of different courses of action, until he gave us the light bulb, an action that each one of us is still grateful for today.

Today millions of people around the world are choosing to take action to stop global warming, and to save the planet in order to ensure that our children have a better future. Every time you choose a paper or cloth bag over a plastic one you are answering a call to action that is a common goal for environmentalists around the world.

To give you my simplest possible definition of action – 'an action is any act committed by us; either mental or physical that brings us closer to our goals in some way'.

Now this is the important part, action can be either physical or mental. Physical action can be defined as any behaviour that we display that can be observed by somebody else. Reading a book about time management is a physical action that you can take to achieve your goal of being an effective manager of time, so is setting your watch 5 minutes early if you are someone who is always 5 minutes late.

Mental actions on the other hand are the thoughts that go on inside your head which cause you to behave a certain way or attract a certain thing into your life. They are the conversations you have with yourself inside your head to either propel you towards your goals or away from them. If I go back to our example of learning to become an effective manager of time – a person who "continuously thinks to themselves – I am always late, I can never be on time", will despite all the alarm clocks in the world, always be just a little late. However if that same person decides to take action and say to themselves "I am always on time, I always have plenty of time to spare", they will find themselves arriving for meetings and appointments on time with less effort and stress for them and all because of the mental action they took to make themselves a better time keeper.

Now in the movie The Secret, we are told that the universe is like a giant unlimited catalogue and we can order anything we want and it will be ours. What most people don't get or forget about this belief is that while it is most certainly true that the universe is our catalogue and we can order whatever it is that we want we must also take action to help the universe fulfil all our orders.

In order to do this you must take the two types of action. You must first take mental action – you need to change your beliefs and imagine yourself achieving the things you want to be, do or have. You also need to take physical action to bring yourself closer to your goals.

The steps to achieving a goal are very much like an invitation to tea. If I said to you right now, why don't you join me at my house for a cup of tea at 5 pm and the only information you have is my address and your address, it might end up being a rather long and confusing drive for you. However if I give you directions beginning from your house and ending at mine, with details like landmarks and road signs to guide you along the way, I am sure you would be in time for a nice hot cuppa. In the same way any goal or dream that we choose for ourselves can be broken down into a smaller set of directions or smaller goals, with landmarks along the way. You need to take action to help you get from one landmark to the next and before you know it –you have arrived at your goal.

Brian Tracy who is one of the most sought after speakers and personal coaches in the world today and many other world-renowned life coaches recommend the following steps to achieving our goals:

1. Write down your goal in specific terms

2. Break your goal down into smaller achievable milestones

3. Take ACTION towards achieving one of those milestones TODAY!

4. Take ACTION towards achieving your goals EVERY SINGLE DAY!

The key message here is ACTION is equal to ACHIEVEMENT so take ACTION today!

In your accompanying work book you will find a very helpful exercise on Action to help you along your journey of the A-Z mastery.

BELIEF

The next step I want to talk to you about on our journey on the A-Z of Mastery is BELIEF. In order to achieve mastery over yourself and your life you must first have belief that you can indeed achieve this mastery. So what exactly is belief? Is it faith? Is it desire? Neither of those answers are exact - beliefs are in fact the assumptions we make about ourselves, about our world, about the people we interact with and about how we expect things to be, our beliefs are what shape our thoughts, our conversations and our behaviours.

So why is belief so important? Michael Korda one of the most influential publishers and authors of his time said "To succeed, we must first believe we can". Belief is one of the key ingredients that distinguish achievers from ordinary people –let's discuss some examples.

Lance Armstrong went on to achieve greatness in his life not once but many times over because he 'Believed he could' despite what medical experts and people around him said. Lance Armstrong is the only person to have won the Tour De France seven times despite being diagnosed with cancer.

Henry Ford was told by his engineers countless times that a horse-powered vehicle could not move on its own account without the horses, yet he 'believed' it was possible – we see his belief on the street every day. Nobody other than the 'Wright brothers' who are credited with inventing and building the first air plane, believed that human beings flying through the air was possible. Yet countless air planes fly people across the world today. I could give you thousands of similar examples, both from history and present day. However the main point of all these examples is this – if you believe it – you will ultimately create your belief.

Nikos Kazantzak the famous Greek writer and philosopher said it very well when he said "By believing passionately in something that does not yet exist, we create it". However, and this point is important - belief by itself is not enough – you must have passion for that belief, you must put your heart and soul into that belief to manifest it. Your belief should burn so brightly that you could light a bonfire with it. That is the sort of powerful belief that creates realities. Frank Lloyd Wright – the American architect, interior designer, and writer, said "The thing always happens that you really believe in; and the belief in a thing makes it happen."

So what should we believe in? I know that it's not enough to say that we must believe – we must also know what to believe in and most importantly how to teach ourselves to believe in these things and how to make that belief a strong passionate manifesting belief that changes our reality.

First of all, we must believe in ourselves. I always with passion tell people in my coaching classes that all change begins with you. So before you can even think about changing your beliefs about the world around you – you must first change your beliefs about yourself!

This is a good time to think about your beliefs about yourself – are they positive or negative? Do they inspire you to become a better person or do they make you feel miserable or uncertain about yourself? Do you believe you are a unique, talented individual with something special to offer the world? Do you believe that you deserve to be happy? To be loved? To be wealthy? To be healthy? Do you believe that you have the right to do the work you love every day? Do you believe in your capabilities as a person? Do you believe you are smart, confident, an achiever, or an innovator? What are your beliefs? Turn to the belief section in the accompanying workbook to help you complete this exercise and really work on your self belief.

Now just to show you how belief equals reality I want you to look at your answers to these two questions. Do you believe you deserve to be wealthy – and I mean a really true, fire-lighting belief? If you said NO - chances are you are not satisfied with your finances and life is a bit of a struggle. If you gave a resounding YES, then you are probably already satisfied with your current financial situation or you are well on your way to achieving it.

Now look at this question - Do you believe that you have the right to do the work you love every day? If you said yes – are you doing what you love right now, or are you actively looking for work that you love doing? And if you answered no – then are you miserable in your current job or wish that things could be better?

Once you believe that you are truly capable of achieving greatness and mastery in your life, you must then believe in these goals and in your dreams. Anatole France the French poet and novelist, said "To accomplish great things, we must not only act, but also dream; not only plan, but also believe." You must believe whole-heartedly in your dreams and your goals in order to make them your reality. You must believe that your dreams or goals are achievable, worthwhile and important, and most importantly you must believe that you are capable of achieving them and that you deserve to achieve them.

No man is an island and this holds true for those of us who would like to achieve mastery in our lives. To be true masters, you need also to learn how to interact with the people around you, many of whom are so vital to you achieving your dreams and goals. So thirdly, you need to believe in the people around you. We must believe that people are essentially good, that the good we do comes back to us ten-fold, that people want to help us out, want to be kind to us and want to support us. I love this quote by Rudyard Kipling "I always try to believe the best of everybody – it saves so much trouble". Put this belief to the test the next time you go out shopping for groceries, on one trip continuously tell yourself that all salespeople are wonderful, kind people who only have your best intentions are heart. On the other – convince yourself that sales people are rude, arrogant individuals whose sole purpose in life is to make your existence miserable. Did the salespeople you encountered act in accordance with your belief? I have tried this exercise and I am amazed at how my belief translates into my reality.

Lastly you need to believe in the Universe and believe that the universe exists to fulfil your dreams and your goals, and that whatever you order from the cosmic catalogue will ultimately be delivered to you when you believe it enough. Believe in the power of belief.

Now that we've talked about what we should believe in, the next question is how do we change our beliefs to reflect that? We said earlier that beliefs are our thoughts about things/people/ourselves, so in order to change our beliefs – we have to change our....you guessed it – THOUGHTS!

So the first thing you need to do is identify all the thoughts that are in CONFLICT with your beliefs about your dreams and your goals and replace them with thoughts that are in accordance with them. You also need to identify the reasons why you continuously believe a particular thought and replace that with reasons that support your belief instead.

For example if I believe that I will always be overweight because I am 10 pounds overweight at the moment, then in order to change that belief, I must believe that I can be my desired weight and have a healthy, fit body. I can believe this, if I give myself reasons such as – I have lost weight before, thousands of people just like me are losing 10 pounds every year. In short I eliminate all my mental arguments which are convincing me not to believe in my goal. Instead I focus on those thoughts that are in-line with my goal.

To summarize, I will use this quote "All personal breakthroughs begin with a change in beliefs" by Anthony Robbins who is a master of peak performance.

The mastery exercise in Belief in your workbook will help you apply this secret effectively in your daily life.

COURAGE

The letter 'C' in this program the A-Z of mastery stands for three things, so it's more like the three C's of mastery – Courage, Confidence and Commitment.

First let's talk about Courage, before you can even begin to achieve your goals or dreams, you must first have the courage to dream and to put those dreams into action.

Do you remember learning how to ride a bike? It took tremendous courage on the part of your younger self to take those wheel stabilisers off the bike and attempt to balance without them. You knew you were going to fall a few times and you knew you might end up with a few cuts and bruises along the way. Yet you still went ahead and took off those stabilisers in order to achieve your goal of being able to ride a bike without the help of stabilisers, or help of a parent. Your desire to learn how to ride a bike was so strong that it gave you the courage to face your fears of falling down and getting hurt and allowed you to ultimately attain your goals

Muhammad Ali said it very well when he said "He who is not courageous enough to take risks will accomplish nothing in life". And if we talk about a man with extraordinary courage it is but natural to talk about Nelson Mandela, who was imprisoned for 27 years as a result of his fight against apartheid and the South African Government. After nearly three decades of hard labour and imprisonment he was finally released and the country held its first multi-racial election in 1994 in an effort to end racial segregation. Nelson Mandela's extra-ordinary courage, confidence and commitment were vital factors in helping him attain his goals, and he went on to win the Nobel Peace Prize and become South Africa's first black president.

Do you have a dream or a goal or a desire that you wish to achieve in your life? What are some of the reasons that prevent you from achieving them? Is one of those reasons courage? Are you afraid of taking the plunge, of believing in your dreams and your abilities; are you afraid of what people will say or what will happen? Is it the absence of courage that is preventing you from achieving your life's dreams?

Mark Twain said "Courage is resistance to fear, mastery of fear, not absence of fear". It is important that we remember this the next time we feel fear when making a decision or choosing a path for ourselves. It is but normal to feel fear. Once you recognize that this is a normal part of the process it makes it much easier to master this fear and commit and stay with your decision.

So I encourage you to have courage from today to follow your passion, to live your dreams and to make your goals a reality.

CONFIDENCE

The second C stands for confidence. When you walk into a room full of people you can easily identify the ones with extraordinary confidence from the ones without this confidence. They are the people who walk tall and stand proud, who are making conversation with everyone around them, and holding people spellbound with their stories. There is something about a person with confidence; it makes others want to talk to them, listen to their ideas and buy into their dreams or ideas.

So where does this confidence come from? Confidence comes from the belief that you are a unique and special individual with something wonderful to offer the world. It comes from knowing what you excel at and believing in your own strengths and abilities. People with confidence know both their strengths and their weaknesses. However they prefer to focus their energies on their strengths and special qualities which make them extraordinary.

Roderick Thorp famous for writing Nothing Lasts Forever which was filmed later as Die Hard said "We have to learn to be our own best friends because we fall too easily into the trap of being our own worst enemies." This means to resist being your own self critic.

You must also have confidence in your ability to achieve your goals. If your goal is to write an award winning novel and you believe that you can't write very well, then you probably won't be getting published any time in the near future. In the words of Vincent van Gogh "If you hear a voice within you say 'you cannot paint', and then by all means paint and that voice will be silenced." The very process of taking action and defying the inner voice will manifest immense reward.

There is a wonderful exercise in your workbook to help you improve your confidence in ten simple steps. Confidence fortunately is not a genetic trait and is a skill that you can learn easily and improve on all your life.

One of the most wonderful displays of confidence that I have encountered is from a young boy named Edward J McGrath Jr who was featured in Chicken Soup for the Soul by Jack Canfield and Mark Victor Hanson. Edward J McGrath had an exceptional view on life – here is his story.

"'I'm not old enough to play baseball or football. I'm not eight yet. My mom told me when you start baseball, you aren't going to be able to run that fast because you had an operation. I told Mom I wouldn't need to run that fast. When I play baseball, I'll just hit them out of the park. Then I'll be able to walk."

COMMITMENT

The third C is Commitment; you must be committed to your goals and to achieving mastery in your life. Finding a goal to believe in is only half the battle won. You must be committed to taking action each and every day to bring you closer to your goals. Commitment however is easier said than done. When I am coaching people I always listen very carefully to the language that they use. I have discovered that people have varying levels of commitment. People may say ' I'll try' 'I wish' 'I should' 'I hope' 'I want' 'I need' 'I have to' 'I may' 'I can' 'I will' 'I must'. The level of commitment is paramount to mastery and success. Commitment must have no built in failure. A person who is 100% committed will take action and achieve their goals. The very definition of Commitment says that "it is the act of binding yourself either emotionally, physically or intellectually to a course of action".

Thomas Edison said "The successful person makes a habit of doing what the failing person doesn't like to do."

Let's take an example, let's say you are committed to leading a fit and healthy life – however to do this you need to ensure that you do many things, some which you may not enjoy doing at all. In order to stay fit and healthy you may need to

- Workout everyday
- Wake up earlier or sleep later

- Give up certain food that you love eating
- Give up alcohol
- Restrict your social life
- Control your diet and watch what you eat

Now you may not enjoy doing any or all of these things every day, but research shows that the fit and healthy people who lose weight and keep it off are the ones that are committed to their goals each and every day.

These two masters said it best.

"The men who have succeeded are men who have chosen one line and stuck to it." Andrew Carnegie who was one of the greatest industrialists and philanthropists of his time.

"I have nothing to offer but blood, toil, tears and sweat." Winston Churchill, the British Prime Minister who was well known for his leadership.

These three C's are essential in your aspiration of mastery and some great exercises are in your work book.

DISCIPLINE

After the three C's we have D for Discipline...a word that conjures up images of strict parents and cramming for exams. A word we thought was only associated with our secondary school lives and the military and not successful or accomplished people.

Why do you need discipline in your life? Discipline is the stronger cousin of commitment. Discipline is doing things you don't like or don't have too in order to achieve your long-term goals. It is choosing long-term results over short-term pleasures. Or motivating yourself strongly enough so that you are carrying out the actions to move you towards your long term goals.

I would like to take a few minutes here to share with you the theory of motivation and mastery. There are four stages on the road to mastery.

In stage 1 called obligation – we must be extremely high on discipline. This is the stage when we feel "I should" do something to achieve my goals. In this stage most of your motivation is from external factors which is why your discipline levels should be highest. If I take this example of running to get healthy "I should lose weight and be fit and therefore run every day to achieve this goal".

Stage 2 or desire based motivation is the- "I want to stage" – this is when we start to focus more on the goals we want to achieve. "I want to get healthy" is what drives me to run every day. However you would still need to be very disciplined at this stage.

Stage 3 is enjoyment based motivation or the "I love to" stage This is when you love what you are doing so much that you get lost in the activity, runners often describe this as the runners high, in this stage your discipline levels are lower because much of your motivation is internal and comes from within. The discipline is automaticly replaced for the love of what you are doing.

Stage 4 is mastery or the "I'm inspired, just try and stop me stage". This is when the activity ceases to become an activity and becomes a way of life instead – this is when we achieve mastery. There is very little discipline in this stage and your motivation is almost entirely internal.

Remember that to get from stage 1 to stage 4, it takes DISICPLINE, and lots of it. Mastery does not have a schedule. It cannot be said that you will go from stage 1 to stage 4 in 30 days, it depends on what you are mastering and is different for each individual.

I read somewhere that every worthwhile accomplishment has a price tag attached to it. The question is - are you willing to pay the price to obtain it? You will have to pay for it through your hard work, through sacrifice, through moments of self-doubt and through self-discipline. So you first look at your goals and judge for yourself if they are worth the price tag attached to them, and then you must have the discipline to follow through to achieve them.

Now I know you are probably thinking - how do we incorporate discipline into our lives? Napoleon Hill author of 'Think and Grow Rich' said "Self-discipline begins with the mastery of your thoughts. If you don't control what you think, you can't control what you do."

So an essential step along our journey to mastery is to have discipline over our thoughts and to think only those thoughts that will bring us closer to our goals.

At the beginning of your workbook you write out actions that you need to take to bring you closer to your goals. Discipline is what will ensure that you take action each and every day to bring you closer to your goals and to achieving mastery.

Let's look at those actions again, identify which ones you need discipline to help you perform them; these are the ones you have to consciously focus on in order to do them each and every day.

In order to become more disciplined in your life these are some steps that will help you along the way.

Step 1: write down your goals in clear and simple language

Step 2: Identify your motivation behind these goals

Step 3: Build habits around your goals, by doing the same thing at the same time every day.

Step 4: Make to – do lists for yourself and stick to them

Step 5: Do not be discouraged by slips and minor setbacks, recognize that it is all part of the process.

It is also important to share another benefit of being disciplined. People who have mastered this key to success easily experience self-growth and spiritual growth. Discipline also gives you more control over your daily life, helps improve your habits and behaviour and is one of the keys to your success.

In order to stay disciplined you need also 'Know your excuses'. Recognising and overcoming your excuses will master your self-discipline. In your workbook there is an exercise on Discipline and Identifying excuses.

EDUCATION

E stands for Education, and by education I do not mean the academic education you may have been through when you were younger, although this too is important. Education in the A – Z of Mastery means long-term continuing education throughout your entire life.

Education is a two-fold path. First you must have the desire to learn. One of the differences between adult and child learners is that adult learners need to be motivated to learn something; they need to want to learn a particular topic before they can fully pay attention to the course. Another way that coaches like myself put it - is that adult learners need to know the "What's in it for me" or the WIIFM of attending the course. What benefit will a particular piece of training or knowledge have on their lives? How will it enrich their lives or make it better?

Many people already have the quest for knowledge and are lifelong learners. It is likely if you bought this course that you are one of those people who chose to better their lives by learning new things and exposing themselves to different ideas. However if you are someone who is a bit hesitant to attempt new ideas or learn new things, you may want to identify your WIIFM before you start. For example if you want to learn a new language – your WIIFM may be to visit that country someday, or read novels in that language, once you have a reason in mind for what you are doing it becomes a lot easier to go ahead and do it.

There are many ways to make education a life-long habit and another step along your journey to mastery. If you study or read about the lives of many great masters and thinkers you will see one common thread running through each of them. They all spent a great deal of time learning and educating themselves.

No course on mastery would be complete without a reference to the greatest master of all time Leonardo Da Vinci. In addition to being a famous painter, and sculptor; he was also a renowned poet, scientist, mathematician, inventor, engineer, anatomist, architect, botanist, musician and writer. It is hard to imagine that he lacked any formal education and he taught himself all these things either through observation and practice or through the process of self-discovery. Leonardo da Vinci is thought to be the most diversely talented person to have ever lived; he is also a man who exemplifies the spirit of continuous education through his talents and feats.

Which brings us to another point, education need not be in a formal setting. You do not have to go back to school or university in order to continue your education, although that certainly is an option. Across the world there are many affordable and exciting courses on offer for adults who wish to pursue their formal education at any level. There are many courses offered by the world's leading universities, some like the Massachusetts Institute of Technology offer a free online open university where anybody and everybody can watch videos of courses and follow the same syllabus that is taught in the classroom. You can choose from most of the undergraduate and graduate courses taught at MIT and all you need is an internet connection and a computer.

Another way to educate yourself is to read books on a particular subject or books by great masters and experts in your area of interest. Did you know that in order to complete a PhD thesis a PhD student must read approximately 50 books on his chosen subject?

It stands to reason that if you read 50 books in a year on a subject of your choosing you will have the same knowledge as a person with a PhD in that subject. Most of us can manage to read 50 books every 2 years, so in theory you can earn a PhD in a different subject every two years for the rest of your life. Imagine how helpful this kind of depth and knowledge will be to you in your life.

A fabulous woman I met during one of my courses told me the secret to living a varied and interesting life. Every single year she and her partner pick a different hobby to master. This way throughout the year they have something new to share with their family and friends and each other and they learn something new every single year. I thought this was one of the best ideas I have ever heard. Imagine learning something new every single year.

A year is enough time to become really good at something. At the end of your life you would have learnt so much and have so many experiences to draw on and share.

If you don't like to read and many people don't, then there are many other options available to you. Audio courses like this one are great for people who don't like to read, and also for people with little time. You can just load the course into your player or play it in your car on the way to work and you have a way to convert 'dead' time into a learning experience for yourself. Today many books and non-fiction bestsellers have been converted into audio books which can be downloaded easily into your portable player or computer. Zig Ziglar one of the greatest sales people of all time, and a very inspirational writer and speaker often talks about the power of listening to motivational tapes and books in your car. This was a habit Zig cultivated when he was a door to door salesman in the early 60's and he found that listening to these tapes always had a positive impact on his sales and performance. Many of these tapes generated new ideas for him to implement in his work and life.

The internet has made knowledge more accessible than ever before. You can enrol yourself in hundreds of courses that are available to you on the internet. Some of them are simple courses using sound and word files, others are more complex and have videos and webinars and other technologies that make it interesting and engaging. There are programs for every interest. Many of them are created by masters in that field, which are packaged and sold online. Many of them include CD's and workbooks like this course or accompanying eBooks for you to read and study.

You can also attend lectures and talks given by people in subject areas that are of interest to you. Alternatively you can find yourself a coach or a mentor, who can teach you about something that he or she is already a master in. Many successful people around the world have coaches or mentors who help them learn and stretch themselves. Issac Newton said "If I can see more than others it is because I have stood on the shoulders of giants". We can only presume he was talking about his coaches, mentors, masters and teachers.

Experience also is a great educator if there is something you wish to learn. However if you do not want to attend a course or read a book, perhaps you could be like Leonardo Da Vinci and learn from experience.

It is often said that "Knowledge is power", education is the key to that power and power is part of the package that is mastery. Your workbook has in-depth mastery exercise on Education.

CHAPTER FOUR

FROM FORGIVENESS TO JOY

FORGIVENESS

The first F you and I will look at is Forgiveness. Now considering it is said that the human mind has around 70,000 thoughts a day it is really important that the thoughts you focus on are for the good of all that you wish to manifest in your life. Imagine if your mind had no inhibiting thoughts and you started with a clean slate today! Moreover, you could start to place any thought you wished to in your mind right now! What would you start with? What would you really, really be focusing on? Just like the catalogue of the Universe, you can create your own internal catalogue right now! In order to do this and make a fresh start the Forgiveness process is essential. Only when you truly forgive will you make the transformations which will make the difference that makes the difference. Forgiveness starts with self forgiveness then forgiveness of anybody else in your life who has hurt you or caused you pain of any kind. This could be family members, teachers, close partners, business partners, work colleagues etc. I can not over emphasise the importance of forgiveness.

Learn the lesson, forgive and move on. I mean really and truly forgive. This will not mean to condone or to say who was right or wrong. Unconsciously you will have experienced a situation from a program. That program can be changed. What has happened is not as important as the meaning in which you have attached to it. Change the meaning. Resentments, fears and pain of any kind are a burden upon you and will weigh you down. They can become toxic and cause you further physical and mental pain and anguish. This is a heavy price to pay. Let go and release yourself of any anxieties. The clearing work that you do with forgiveness will change you on an unconscious level. You become freer, lighter, happier, peaceful and relaxed. Forgiveness is powerful. Mastering forgiveness is empowering and liberating. Life takes on a renewed meaning. Transformations take place as you now focus on what you really do want in your life. Begin with your clean slate NOW. Start now to fill the catalogue of your mind with only positive thoughts that will lead you to your goals and life purpose.

FOCUS

Many of the people I have coached have commented that I am a really focused person and in turn they feel they can and want to emulate my focus. I am focused on my clients' success as their success is as important to me as it is to them. Now just imagine for a minute that you are a world famous race car driver; you are sitting in the driver's seat of an amazingly powerful machine, travelling faster than you ever have in your life. Every muscle in your body is straining to control your vehicle and the world is rushing by at breakneck speed. A wrong move at this time would be fatal. Would you at this point in time be focusing on the race track ahead and reaching the finishing line or would you be looking at the crowds, the sidelines and everywhere else?

A race car driver would not hesitate before answering 'focus on the race-track ahead'. Indeed pure focus is what keeps him on the track and away from the pitch and the sidelines and a possible accident. The first rule of focus is this: "Wherever you are, be there". (Author unknown).

Peter McWilliams a best-selling author of self-help books said "Our thoughts create our reality - where we put our focus is the direction we tend to go." Thus the power of focus on the path to mastery is simple. The more you focus on mastery and on your goals, the closer you will move towards your goals and the faster you will achieve mastery.

Imagine for a minute that your mind is like a computer and just like a computer it is bombarded with hundreds of programs, requests, and other processes. Focus is the mouse which selects the program that our computer (mind) will run and we will perform accordingly. If you do not consciously control your mouse, it may pick programs that are useless or detrimental to you. However if you choose the right programs then you will perform the right tasks and actions at the right times.

A true master is able to focus his mouse on the right program almost all the time and with little effort. Like all mastery this ability to focus on something like a laser beam comes with effort and a lot of practice.

Anthony Robbins who has famously been an advisor to American leaders has much to say on the subject of focus.

"It's not what's happening to you now or what has happened in your past that determines who you become. Rather, it's your decisions about what to focus on, what things mean to you, and what you're going to do about them that will determine your ultimate destiny."

"One reason so few of us achieves what we truly want is that we never direct our focus; we never concentrate our power. Most people dabble their way through life, never deciding to master anything in particular."

Focus allows you to free up your time, do things that are important to you and achieve important results in your life.

In the movie The Secret, it was said that whatever we focus on expands and grows. So if you focus on the fact that you have no money, it is likely that this thought will grow and expand and become your reality. On the other hand if you focus on the fact that you have enough, it is likely that you will always have enough to pay your bills and meet your expenses. Now what do you think could happen if you focus on - you have more than enough money and you have an abundance of money as there is plenty to go round?

Brian Tracy said "The key to success is to focus our conscious mind on things we desire not things we fear."

One excellent way to focus your thoughts is to write them down. The act of writing down a goal or an action is an excellent way to focus your mind to carry out that task. Another way is to constantly talk to yourself inside your head. We all have thoughts in our heads all the time; did you know that you can choose your thoughts? You can focus on running a particular thought through your head at any point in time. Let's do it now with this thought "I am on my way to mastery and I will do everything to achieve mastery", now repeat it 5 times, 10 times. It may seem strange at first, consciously focusing your thoughts. However, like all things that are practised the more you do something the easier it becomes to do.

Sun Tzu the ancient Chinese military general and strategist said it very well in his quote of Focus "Opportunities multiply as they are seized". Focusing on the opportunities that come your way will only multiply them.

FAITH

F also stands for Faith. Put simply faith is the absence of doubt. Do you doubt your abilities, how great you can be or whether you can achieve mastery. Faith is the anecdote to this doubt. When you doubt yourself, your abilities or your goals you subconsciously tell yourself that you are not capable enough of achieving your goals, and as you believe it becomes your reality. This is why faith is so important in achieving mastery and the lack of faith is the number one reason for our limitations.

Faith is the third cog in the wheel that is made up of Action and Belief. Faith is what allows you to turn your beliefs into actions. Without faith you would not be able to overcome obstacles and limitations, without faith you would be unable to achieve your goals and ideas.

There are three key areas for you to develop your faith; firstly you must have faith in your abilities to achieve the things you want to achieve. Secondly you must have faith in your goals and ideas and lastly you must have faith in the things you believe in order to make them a reality.

How do you make faith an integral part of your life? Many teachers of faith have found that using positive affirmations and thoughts are a key tool in helping you build up faith. These thoughts and affirmations influence the sub-conscious mind in a positive way which ultimately produces good thoughts and subsequently leads to good actions. When thoughts are constructive they become alive with vitality and expand and develop into creativity which often results in inspired action.

Sir William Osler the great Canadian physician said that "Without faith a man can do nothing; with it all things are possible."

Remember how we talked about internal and external motivation when we were talking about Discipline? Well faith is a huge part of that internal motivation that ultimately leads you to mastery. Allow faith to become your relentless driver.

Helen Keller who was the first deaf and blind person to earn a bachelors degree and someone who subsequently became an author and a lecturer said that "Optimism is the faith that leads to achievement. Nothing can be done without hope and confidence." Helen went from a life of darkness to a world where she learned to communicate with the outside world.

Your work book provides more on Forgiveness, Focus and Faith to help you on your road to mastery.

GOALS

No program on mastery would be complete without a discussion on goals and the importance of setting them. The difference between a dream and a goal is that dreams are often fleeting, or merely passing wishes that we do not work towards either consciously or unconsciously, while a goal is a specific, measurable achievement which you work towards sometimes both consciously and unconsciously.

Talk to any master and he or she will tell you the importance of Goal setting. While working on this program, I came across an article which stated that one of the traits of millionaires is that they set clear, specific goals and they write them down. This process of writing down your goals is what is most important. It has been established that there is a definite connection between your subconscious mind and the act of writing something down versus merely thinking it. Writing your goals down will help your sub-conscious mind manifest it faster than if you merely focussed on thinking about your goal in your head. Writing down your goal also helps you consciously work towards what you desire.

While each person's goal is as diverse and different as he or she is, all well written goals have certain characteristics in common. They are specific, measurable, obtainable, challenging, and have a completion date attached. Though most business books stress on the importance of a goal being obtainable, in mastery we choose to define obtainable as anything which can be obtained by the universal catalogue.

We can set career goals, financial goals, family goals, physical goals – about how you want to feel and look, educational goals, personal goals, spiritual goals, creative goals, or any other kind of goals that are important to you in your life.

Goals are like a compass; they point us in the right direction and motivate us to turn our picture of our ideal future into a reality. They also help us to stay focussed and not lose sight of what is important to us in the long run.

Accomplishing and achieving your goals, also helps build self-confidence and motivates you to achieve more of the goals you set for yourself. Take for example if I set a goal to lose 10 pounds over the next two months, I will be more motivated to stick to my goal if I lose a pound or so in the first week of the program. This minor achievement will motivate me to achieve more of my goal.

Now let us share together the way to set goals. First it is important to set your lifetime goals, those things that you want 10 or more years into the future. It is important that you set goals for all aspects of your life to ensure that you have a balanced coverage of things that are important to you. At this point you may not be able to envision how you are going to achieve these goals. It does not matter, pen them down anyway. You can then whittle down these goals into a 5 year plan, a one year plan, a 6 month plan and finally a one month plan, which are the goals you will work on right NOW. You can then create a daily to-do list to ensure you achieve your goals for the month. This technique is fabulous for achieving goals we can envision achieving easily, such as career goals and educational goals.

However if you have goals that you cannot write a plan for, or cannot envision a time frame for your goal, you may want to set goals using the techniques from the law of attraction. For this you must write your goals down as if you already have achieved them and they must be written in positive language. Very often when a client first comes to me for coaching they will begin to tell me what they DO NOT want. They may for instance say "I do not want to be unhappy" "I do not want to fail again" "I do not want this to happen again". I ask them if they want MORE in their life of what they DO NOT want. Puzzled they always say "Well, No, of course not". Right there and then I ask them to stop inviting what they DO NOT WANT into their life. I very quickly ask them what they DO want. Usually they are quiet as they start to access their thoughts. Changing their thought process is the beginning of a transformation. Now, this following point is very important so listen with great care. Our sub-conscious does not register the words 'Do – not'. So 'I want to be overweight' and 'I do not want to be overweight' register as exactly the same thing – the desire to be overweight. It is vital to understand and remember that you do NOT focus on what you DO NOT want. Focus on what you DO want, the desired result. Be focused on the outcome you want. I always ensure that my client's goals are positive, personal, present, possible for them, performance related, penned down – the golden rule of the six 'P's.

An example of a well written goal using this technique is this: "I, Jacky have a wonderful relationship with all my clients and help make a positive impact on each one of their lives". Notice that the goal is written using an 'I' statement, and also as if I have already achieved my goal. This language enables the universe to manifest my goal here and now. Write your goals using language that is positive and in the present tense to help manifest your goals more quickly as the universe works to make it come true.

Teachers of the law of attraction say that writing a goal once and forgetting it is not enough. You must read your written goals three times a day or more in order for your sub-conscious to register it and manifest it. And you have to do this process every single day – that is you cannot miss a day for it takes at least 30 days for the registration to take place and still continue to do this after the 30 days. I cannot over emphasize the importance of doing this! For the brain has a reticular activating system which acts as a filter for all of your senses and all that you think and ask for. Whatever your beliefs are, the filters will match them. Every intention you have therefore has to be positive. This is why your affirmations need to be positively and purposely constructed. Have an affirmation for each and every goal that you set yourself. Affirm what you want as though you already have it with all the emotions that go with it for your intensity of the emotions will also be filtered by your reticular activating system. This belongs to the law of asking, believing and receiving. Also in case you are accustomed to giving yourself talks that contradict these goals, then reading your goals three or more times every single day will eventually replace those negative thoughts with positive ones.

GRATITUDE

G also stands for Gratitude, and gratitude is a fundamental key to the Law of Attraction.

This is what Rhonda Byrne – the author of The Secret has to say about the power of gratitude. "With all that I have read and with all that I have experienced in my own life using The Secret, the power of gratitude stands above everything else. If you do one thing with the knowledge of The Secret, use gratitude until it becomes your way of life..."

Yes gratitude must really become your way of life. If you are not grateful for what you have right now, how can you be grateful for what you may receive in the future? It is impossible to bring more into your life if you are feeling ungrateful about what you have. Why? Because the thoughts and feelings you emit as you feel ungrateful are all negative emotions." That is the message that you send out to the universe. So BE GRATEFUL NOW. Start RIGHT NOW. Be grateful for the food you have, the bed you sleep in, the house you live in, the car that you drive. Make the list endless. Be full of gratefulness.

Why is gratitude such a powerful tool? Gratitude is the expression of a positive emotion that we feel in relation to a goal. Gratitude allows you to accept and acknowledge the value of something in your life. When you accept the value of something- you stop resisting it and it becomes real in your life. Gratitude is a tool when used correctly can help you manifest the things that you want into your life.

Many teachers of the law of attraction have different ways of using the power of gratitude in their lives. Here are some of their techniques.

1. Practice being grateful for 3 minutes every morning. As soon as you wake up, list 10 things you are grateful for that day.

2. Start a gratitude journal. Every day write down five things that you are grateful for today. Make this a part of your to-do list so that you don't forget. The 5 things must be 5 different things every single day. Never duplicate anything.

3. My favourite technique is this. After practising writing a gratitude journal for about 2 weeks, start writing two pages. On one page lists 5 things you are grateful for right now, and the other page list things you are imagining that you are grateful for in your future life. What a great way to manifest the things you want. This can be quite powerful too.

The exercise on how to use the power of gratitude in your life every day is in your workbook.

HOLISTIC APPROACH

We now move on to H – for a Holistic Approach. A holistic approach means taking into account all aspects of yourself, your body, mind, emotions, and spirit. When you adopt a holistic approach to life you focus your energy and power on all the aspects that make up you – that is your mind, your emotions, your desires and your intentions. In the holistic approach we acknowledge that all aspects of our body, mind and spirit are interconnected and that we need to spend our time and energy strengthening each of these facets of our lives in order to live a full and balanced life. Some ways to incorporate a holistic lifestyle is to eat greener, or eat more organic and natural foods, or learn and practice yoga and meditation and exercise on a daily basis. If you want proof of the existence of the mind-body connection, think of the last time you went for a ten minute walk or run. How did you feel? Did you feel better not only on a physical level but also mentally, are you more relaxed, and calmer and more focussed. You are also probably more energetic which allows you to work faster and better. Exercising also makes you feel happier and more positive, which can have a positive effect on your relationships and the people you interact with. Once you start exercising and you feel the benefits associated with it, you will probably want to do things to maximize that benefit like eating healthier or exercising for longer. So can you see how working on and taking care of one aspect of ourselves can have results in so many other aspects?

Today most doctors and psychologists acknowledge the holistic approach as being the most successful approach to treating many difficult and often fatal conditions. This explains why so many survivors of cancer, including Lance Armstrong focussed not only on their treatment but also on strengthening their mind and body and on staying positive and happy.

Today world class athletes know that half the battle is won in their minds and not only on the sports field and spend as much time meditating, practising yoga and visualizing their success as they do physically practising on the field or in the pool.

To adopt a more holistic approach to living your life you must:

Focus on wellness in your body: this includes exercise, healthy eating, natural medicines and treatments, proper sleep, time to relax and detress, and therapies such as natural wellness therapies and massage therapies.

Focus on wellness in your mind: focus on thinking positive thoughts, on being more optimistic, on enriching your mind through reading or exploring new ideas, on being more creative and meditating or mentally relaxing your mind.

Focus on wellness in emotion: by caring for and nurturing yourself, for acknowledging and dealing with your emotions; by expressing your emotions to people around you and by journalising them or some other form of self expression.

Focus on wellness in spirit: by spending time alone in quiet reflection, enjoying nature, praying or any other type of religious ritual that works for you and by enjoying the moment no matter where you are and what you are doing.

An exercise on incorporating a more holistic approach and health to your life is in your A-Z of Mastery workbook.

HARMONY

The letter H in this program also stands for Harmony which is another key concept in the A-Z of Mastery program. Harmony essentially means being in balance in all the areas of our lives or in other words it is the ABSENCE of discontent or upset in our lives. Opposite to harmony is discord. Harmony must start within us. When we are not in Harmony we experience difficulties in our relationships at work, and at home and this leads to many other feelings like stress, discontent, anger etc.

Before we communicate effectively and develop relationships we must have harmony within ourselves. In order for any group or relationship to work there must be harmony. When minds are in harmony with one another it will be to the benefit of all as the energy vibration is raised with the alliance and co-operation of all. Working towards a specific goal or purpose in harmony will manifest results with universal power and many great things can be mastered and achieved.

Harmony is also viewed as alignment between four key aspects of our lives, these are:

1. What we say – the words we use to talk about things

2. What we think – our thoughts about things and people

3. What we feel - our feelings

4. What we do – our actions

If all these four aspects are in sync with each other, then it can be said that we are in harmony.

We must also evaluate whether we are in harmony in the following areas of our lives:

- Our financial lives
- Career and relationships at work
- Love and intimacy
- Personal environment and organization
- Personal, professional and spiritual development
- Health and Well-being
- Family and Friends
- Recreation and free time.

Let's take the example of money since this is an area that many of us struggle with. If the way you think about money is in conflict with the way you behave with money, or in the way you talk or feel about it, then chances are that you will not be satisfied with your current financial situation. If you program yourself that money is easy to come by and you have lots of it, however you then talk about money in terms of how scarce it is, or behave in a way that is contradictory to how a person with a lot of money would behave, you are in all likelihood going to struggle with your finances.

If you are angry, upset, stressed out, or frustrated then it is likely that you are not in harmony between your thoughts, feelings, actions and words; this also leads you to make unwise and unhealthy decisions, since in a state of disharmony you send yourself mixed messages, the end result of which is a state of confusion and self-doubt.

In a nutshell harmony allows you to be comfortable within your own skin; you then operate from a place of genuineness and integrity, both with yourself and with others around you. It also enables you to live your life with peace and serenity.

I have a fabulous exercise in your work book which will will help you develop harmony within.

INSPIRATION

We now move on to the next phase of our program, the 4 I's in the A-Z of Mastery program. The 4 I's stand for Inspiration, Invincible, Innovation and Imagination.

What is inspiration? The dictionary definition of Inspiration is a condition in which our mind or emotions are stimulated to a high degree of feeling or activity. When you are inspired you are able to create new things and start or complete projects and activities with ease. One can only imagine the degree of inspiration that great masters such as Van Gogh, Beethoven and Leonardo Da Vinci must have had in order to have produced the works of art and music that they did. We all lack motivation from time to time, and it is at this point when our motivation levels are low, that we need to seek inspiration in order to complete our tasks.

The difference between inspiration and motivation is simple; motivation may be both internal and external. However inspiration is always self-generated and the need to act always comes from within you. Let me share a secret with you, in order to develop this program I needed to be inspired. There were days when I sat down at my desk and was unable to write, and the slightest thought or interruption was enough to make me stray from my desk. However there were an equal number of days when I could not wait to sit down at my computer and start typing away, I would barely stop for food or drink; I would barely even stop to think before putting my thoughts onto the system. Some days I would even wake up in the middle of the night, and have to rush to my system in order to say what needed saying. Inspiration is what helped me turn this program on Mastery into a reality.

On the days that I was not inspired to write, I could not sit back and relax, I had deadlines and commitments, so I had to find ways to inspire myself in order to meet those deadlines and commitments. These are some of my favourite ways to get inspired to do what needs doing. You may have other things that work for you, so feel free to experiment and explore until you figure out what works best.

More details are available in your A-Z of Mastery workbooks.

1. Look for new experiences

2. Keep an open mind

3. Pay attention to your emotions

4. Share your experiences

5. Schedule some 'me' time

6. Look to your role models

7. Follow your faith

8. Exercise and move

INVINCIBLE

'I' also stands for Invincible, and by Invincible I don't mean invincible like Superman, although that would be certainly be fabulous. Instead we mean that we should aim to have an 'invincible' spirit, or a spirit which cannot be defeated, a spirit that is unconquerable despite the hardships, adversities and trials we might face throughout our lives.

Thomas Fuller the 17C British writer and clergyman said this about being invincible, "An invincible determination can accomplish almost anything and in this lies the great distinction between great men and little men."

In order to be invincible, you must first seek self-knowledge, since only when you know yourself intimately can you be strong enough to over-come all hardship. You must be intimately familiar with all your successes and your failures.

Secondly, you must love yourself; only if you love yourself enough do you become invisible to the on slaughter of others and also the constant bombardment from the media, which urges us to be thinner, taller, richer, or better looking.

You need to also have the courage to follow your dreams despite criticism from others and the blocks and obstacles which you have to work on your journey to success and mastery.

The exercise in your workbook will guide you on how to be invincible.

INNOVATION

Innovation is another key to mastery that begins with an 'I'. In order to achieve mastery and to achieve your goals it certainly helps if you develop your innovative skills. Innovation and Invention are two different things; invention means bringing into being something that has never been before, innovation means newer and better ways of doing things.

The first personal computer ever to be built was an invention, anything that followed after that was an innovation.

You don't need to be a scientist and engineer to be innovative; you can find newer and better ways of doing things in our day to day lives. Being innovative on a daily basis, means coming up with new ways to serve your meal leftovers for example, or new ways to get everything done in your day. Practise new ways on a daily basis to form the habit of innovation. You can be innovative at work, at home and with your relationships with people.

At work you fill find that innovative people are often considered the most valuable. Many companies today list the concept of innovation as one of their core values, and so you can see why it pays to develop an innovative mindset.

In order to be innovative, allow yourself to be creative, and take steps to incorporate creativity into our daily lives. Whether it is by painting a picture, writing in a journal or taking up a hobby like pottery or craft making or it could be new ways to create wealth into your life.

Innovators always ask themselves questions about how to make something better, faster, cheaper, is there a more effective way of doing something? Can something else be used in its place? Can it serve another purpose? Walt Disney said it well in his quote on innovation "Whenever I go on a ride, I'm always thinking of what's wrong with the thing and how it can be improved. "

One of the most essential tools for being innovative is keeping a notebook to note down ideas, thoughts, stories, quotes, pictures and other inspirations.

Tap into your creative side with the exercises in your workbook.

IMAGINATION

Lastly 'I', stand for imagination. Imagination is the ability to form a mental image of something that is not perceived by any of our five senses.

Every single person already has the ability to imagine. In some people however it is more strongly developed than in others.

Creative people often find it easy to imagine things in their minds eye, and it is no secret that whatever the human mind can conceive it can then go on to make a reality. Albert Einstein once said "Imagination is more important than knowledge. For while knowledge defines all we currently know and understand, imagination points to all we might yet discover and create."

By imagining solutions to problems and situations in our minds, we often find the right solution staring at us in the face. By imagining our perfect day, we often envision our perfect career or job, and by imagining our perfect partners we often recognize them when we meet them.

This program and the life principles we are working on for you to aspire to mastery in your life was once a part of my imagination, before I decided to work towards making it a reality.

Imagination allows us to envision our lives and achievements as we want them to be and then gives us the power to make them into our reality.

Walt Disney is perhaps one of the most famous men who translated his imagination into reality and a multi-million dollar empire; he has this advice to share with us "All your dreams can come true if you have the courage to pursue them."

To help develop your ability to imagine and to learn how to put it to good use follow the exercises in your work books.

JOY

Joy is that feeling of happiness and enthusiasm which you experience when you feel that all is well with your world. When you are joyful you feel enthusiastic, and abundant. When you are full of joy you are also more easily able to attract the things you want into your life.

The law of attraction tells us that we are more easily able to manifest things in our lives if we approach them from a positive emotional reaction. When you are not happy and and you are upset it is unlikely that you will be able to manifest what you want. However when you are happy and joyful, you will find that the universe is more eager to fulfil your wishes.

Being joyful has many benefits. Your relationships will prosper because you will be at your happiest and most giving self. Your health will be better. When you are joyful you are less likely to stress and snap. You will also feel more peaceful and able to cope with challenges in your life. Cultivating joy in your life can be a very valuable tool along your journey to mastery.

Yes you can learn to cultivate joy. While some people seem to have happy and positive lives, many have an equal mix of happy and sad times. However there are some of us who instinctively go in search of things that make us happy, and we look for things that bring us joy. There are others amongst us who see the glass as half full and chose not to cultivate joy and laughter in their lives. Which type of person do you think is happier, more stress free, has better relationships? Which type of person do you want to be?

Joseph Campbell was an American mythologist, writer and lecturer. His philosophy is often summarized by the phrase "Follow your bliss", a sentence we also heard in the movie The Secret. Following your bliss means doing what makes you full of joy inside, and that joy in turn nourishes you and encourages you to achieve more.

The source of much unhappiness for many of us is not being in the right job or the right career. Now a large part of your lives and energy is spent at work and if you are not 'following your bliss' then in all likelihood you are not joyful for a large part of your life.

It is important to do all that you can to follow your bliss in terms of what you would like to do with in your life; do you have a dream of what you would like to do for a living, or how you would like your life to be. In order to follow your bliss, you may have to muster the courage to take the road less travelled and by doing so you may end up finding your bliss. To give you an example of this, a client and friend of mine although he worked for himself in the legal business was not happy in his daily life.

Although he had been successful he felt that he was not really getting the enjoyment that he needed from his work. The law firm he was with had been in the family for several generations and it seemed that it was expected of him to follow in his father's footsteps as had been the case with several generations. So really it was somebody else's bliss he was following. I asked him what he felt was missing. He said that it was his creativity that was stifled. It turned out that his hobby was his real passion which was making hand crafted furniture. He eventually followed his bliss and is now thriving and following his bliss making hand crafted furniture for a living.

I consider myself very lucky to do the work that I love and that brings me joy. I chose to become a person who helps transform people because I realized that working with people and helping them achieve greatness in their lives brings me joy and makes me feel grateful and abundant. However it was not an easy decision to take. It required me to step outside my comfort zone and take a few risks and in the beginning there were many things that I needed to sacrifice or learn to do without. However the journey was much easier because I knew that I was following my bliss. Had I not derived this feeling of joy and happiness from coaching and transforming people, I probably would not have had so much certainty and passion with my decision.

Many of us however may not have the choice of quitting our jobs today. And that may not be the answer for you. After all in order to do so you would need to work out a strategy that is right for you. Yet you can find the things about your current job that you enjoy and which bring you joy. I have also once been in a job like so many have at some time in their life, where attempt as I might, I could not always be happy. There were some areas of the work that did not sit comfortably with my values. It is possible you can relate to this. In that case I had to learn how to find joy in the parts of my work that did sit with my values and also to find joy in areas outside of my work.

It's no coincidence that many of the things that give you inspiration can also be a source of joy. Spending time in nature; spending time with people you love; working on projects that stimulate you can all be valuable sources of joy. Pets can also provide much joy to their owners as they can make good companions.

You can and need to look for ways to make joy a part of your daily ritual if you want to benefit from the law of attraction and use it to manifest the things that you want in your life.

More ideas on cultivating joy in your life can be found in your work books

CHAPTER FIVE

FROM KINDNESS TO OMNIPOTENCE

KINDNESS

So we begin with Kindness. I love this following quote. "No kind action ever stops with itself. One kind action leads to another. Good example is followed. A single act of kindness throws out roots in all directions, and the roots spring up and make new trees. The greatest work that kindness does to others is that it makes them kind themselves." Amelia Earhart (Distinguished woman aviator and noted author).

If you are to achieve mastery in your life, you must first learn how to be kind to others and most importantly to ourselves. As Amelia Earhart said, "kindness is like a chain reaction, one kind action leads to another and eventually it all comes back to us tenfold."Now just stop for a moment and think what that would bring into your life. What would you like to come back to you tenfold?

Some people are naturally kind. These are the people we know who can always be counted on for a smile and a kind word. These are the people we all consider gentle and wonderful souls and we enjoy being around them. We can all learn to be that person.

I am a firm believer that before we can start changing the world, we must first start with ourselves. So let's spend a few minutes talking about how we can be kind to ourselves. It is much easier to learn how to be kind to the people and animals we come into contact with than it is to stop beating ourselves up or making ourselves feel guilty on a routine basis.

Let's look at some ways we can be kind to ourselves:

1. So many of us spend time dwelling on the past, wishing that we could change it, or being plagued by doubts or regrets. However there is nothing WE CAN DO to change what has already happened. We can change the meaning we have placed upon it. So LET IT GO and dwell instead on the present and the things that you want in the future. Don't let thoughts about your past prevent you from focussing on your future.

2. Give yourself a break and do one thing at a time, rather than trying to juggle several things at once. When we try to do everything, we end up stressing ourselves out and pile excessive pressure on ourselves. Doing one thing at a time also allows you to focus on that task completely and you will get it done faster and more efficiently.

3. Spend time on yourself. Take out 20 minutes a day to appreciate yourself, relax or meditate. It makes it much easier for us to be kind to others if we are at peace with ourselves. Peace from within will generate kindness.

4. Some problems are just not worth the effort. Such as spending considerable time and effort arguing, convincing or resolving minor problems, which if we are honest with ourselves are not worth it in the long run. If you and your partner have a daily battle about them taking out the rubbish,

accept that they are not going to do it, and do it yourself or have one of the kids take it out. It's probably not worth the stress and negativity.

5. Many of us work or live with people who place unnecessary demands on our time and our energy. We cannot please everybody. It's better to please ourselves and learn how to politely say NO to others when required.

6. Enjoy life and be happy. We have talked about both happiness and joy already in this program. Learn how to be happy and find joy in your life.

Now that you and I have considered how to be kind to ourselves let's talk about how to be kind to people around us. Barbara De Angelis the American Relationship Consultant said that "Love and kindness are never wasted. They always make a difference. They bless the one who receives them, and they bless you, the giver."

Some ways to manifest kindness around us are -

1. Avoid gossip and rumours like the plague Walk away from any gossip sessions or stand up for the person who is being spoken about. Being kind means being kind to someone even when they are not around.

2. Be a good listener

3. Compliment people, but ensure that it is a genuine compliment and that you really mean what you are saying.

4. Be yourself as much as possible not a second rate version of someone else, but a first rate version of you.

5. Perform random acts of kindness. It makes you feel even better than the receiver, buy someone a cup of coffee, take

a friends pet from a walk, visit a lonely elderly person. Find joy in making other people happy.

6. Volunteer or contribute to a charity on a regular basis. Helping other people will make you feel great.

There are some great ideas on Kindness in your A-Z of Mastery workbook, complete them when you are ready.

KARMA

K also stands for Karma. The concept of Karma comes from ancient Hinduism, thought. It was Buddha who explained it best and it is a fundamental part of Buddhist theory and beliefs.

According to the law of Karma, equality between people in terms of who is rich, who is poor, and other aspects of human life, is not merely a function of birth and circumstance. Our present lives are largely influenced by our past lives and the actions in those lives.

According to the law of Karma, which is also known as the law of cause and effect, whatever we do right now in this life will shape the outcome of our future lives. It is like the principle of Kindness. However we believe that whatever Kindness we do in this life, comes back to us in this life. In the law of Karma, any deeds of kindness in this life will have a positive outcome in our future life.

It is accepted that for many of us proof of alternative lifetimes may be a difficult concept or something that we do not believe in. However we can easily believe that everything that we do affects some future outcome in our lives - our present life. That is the life you are living right now. We are a result of what we did yesterday. It is now that we can become enlightened for we are a product of our own thoughts and actions. What will bring you the results you want in your life right now?

Now really consider the following with great care. Being a master means carefully considering your actions and deciding whether you would want this action to come back to you in the near or distant future, and then taking action based on this decision.

LEVERAGE

The dictionary definition of Leverage means using something as a tool to gain power or an advantage. It is being able to exert a greater influence on a situation with the use of a lever. We are going to explore how to Leverage our strengths, the people around us and tools in order to help us achieve our goals. Leverage can be defined as achieving maximum results with minimum effort that is when efficient ways of working are endorsed.

We all have strengths, or certain things that we are good at, things that we do better than anyone else. Maybe you are an excellent writer or singer, or great at business organization. This is your strength. In order to leverage your strengths you must first know what they are. You can list down your strengths in your workbook.

Now think about your goals and the things you want to achieve – how can you leverage your strengths to achieve your goals? What strengths do you already possess can you use to help you find your dream job, get a promotion, open a business or achieve what your goal is?

When we talk about leverage we also talk about the skill to leverage other people, and by leverage we don't mean to 'use' or take advantage of people. Leverage the knowledge of other people to make a difference to your results. Think about your circle of friends and acquaintances, are there people there that can help you achieve your goals? Maybe they already work in your field of interest; maybe they can help you out with a loan; maybe you could enter into a joint venture with them to expand your business? Leverage can be created in your circles of influence. Who can you leverage to achieve the life of your dreams? Your lower value activities can be delegated or outsourced which is what many successful people do. People like helping other people out. Do remember to be thankful to them and to keep any promises you make to them, and also acknowledge the role they had to play in your success.

We need also to also consider the leverage of the power of tools to achieve our goals. We can use productivity tools to get more done in less time; we can automate our businesses and use technology and systems to create leverage; we can leverage the power of the internet to sell to customers across the globe. What tools can you leverage to achieve your goals?

You can spend more time on the subject of leverage in your workbook.

LOVE

No program on mastery and achievement would be complete without a short discussion on 'love'.

The author Franklin once said "Love doesn't make the world go round. Love is what makes the ride worthwhile."

Psychologists will tell you that love ranks right there with the basic human physiological needs of food and shelter. Without love we cannot survive. It is a fundamental human need to love and be loved.

Love and compassion are antidotes to negative emotions such as anger and hatred. A cup of love is the medicine to counteract negative emotions. Without love there is nothing for everything begins with love. No good happens without love. So it makes sense that we must start with love. Everything starts with love. Place love in that space where there is fear, hesitation, procrastination, hate, judgement, neglect, resentment, anger. Notice the change in your thoughts, your insights and your feelings. Love really does change everything. Impregnate thought with love. This is the law of love. Enhance this strength and consciously develop love and compassion so loving-kindness becomes an invincible all encompassing connection.

We cannot discuss all aspects of love in such a short period of time, neither can we discuss ways to love – love is more a conscious choice we make when we accept and rejoice in ourselves and in other people.

We can however together decide and make a conscious choice to have more love in our lives!

In order to have more love in your life you must first decide to accept and love yourself, instead of beating yourself up about things, or finding fault in the way you look or the things you do. Resolve to love yourself instead. Love and accept yourself right now. A technique I use when using Emotional Freedom Therapy on clients is to encourage them to love and accept themselves no matter what.

Louise L Hay the teacher, lecturer and author on self healing recommends a technique to love yourself that is to look yourself in the eye in a mirror every single morning and tell yourself that you love yourself.

I remember a few years ago I attended a Brian Tracy seminar and was told to repeat the following affirmation ten times every single morning as soon as I wake up "I love myself, I love myself, I love myself". Do it. It may seem strange at first. You will get used to it and it certainly beats beating yourself up!

Mae West the famous American actress said it brilliantly when she said "I don't like myself, I am crazy about myself".

Oscar Wilde poetically says "To love oneself is the beginning of a life time romance".

Here is another one of my favourites by an unknown author "You can explore the universe looking for somebody who is more deserving of your love and affection than you are yourself, and you will not find that person anywhere ".

To sum it up I will reference Benjamin Franklin, the American Statesman, scientist, politician, philosopher, writer, printer and inventor – he was most defiantly a true master and inspiring example of achievement and mastery. He once said very rightly "He that falls in love with himself will have no rivals. By loving ourselves, we give others little chance to threaten us or take advantage of any situation".

We must also of course learn to love people in general and not only specific people. We all have people in our lives that we love unconditionally;

however we must also learn to love humanity in general. If we accept and do all that we can and love humanity as a whole, then we tend to have a more optimistic view of the things people do. We are also less likely to get upset and irritated over others actions. Remember the law of love and activate it.

It has been said that successful people love what they do and do what they love. Loving what you do is a critical factor in mastering achievement in your life. In the words of the Talk Show Host, Oprah Winfrey "I've come to believe that each and every one of us has a special calling as unique as a finger print, and that the best way to succeed is to discover what you love and then find a way to offer it to others in the form of a service and work hard".

Now this is a lady who knows what she is talking about for she radiates love in her special calling. Imagine if each and every one of you found your special calling.

Learn more on the subject of love in your workbook.

LEGACY

This naturally leads us onto legacy. Throughout your life you will be moved emotionally by moments of great significance. Think of the great things that have happened in your life time and also throughout history, the moments and the people that you have respected and admired for the great things they have done to create a real lasting legacy on the world or their communities. Without them certain things would not have been achieved. They have made a lasting impact. We have mentioned already in this program many of the famous people who have made a lasting impression on the world. These people not only are remembered for their greatness they truly lived and demonstrated their greatness during their lifetime. They were actually living their legacy.

Now just think about it for a moment what do you really want to be remembered for? What impact do you want to make? What will your legacy be? Then start to live your legacy now. Make every day a significant greatness, one of great importance. Your path will be one of never ending growth, one in which your learning and compassion will be continuing.

MINDSET

The letter M stands for 4 tools that we can use to help us achieve mastery in our lives, the first M stands for mindset or the ability to develop and maintain a positive mindset, M also stands for modelling and magnetic and lastly together we will explore meditation and its usefulness in our lives.

Every experience you have in life is a result of your predominant mental attitude. You have within you the ability to select experiences and impressions that serve you well. It is your choice. You have the ability to shut out all unpleasant and disagreeable experiences. You have the ability to tune into joy, happiness, optimism, success, harmony, peace. Just like a radio station, you can tune into those stations that you like to listen to and raise your positive vibrations. It is your choice. One of the important tools to reaching mastery in our lives is the ability to develop and maintain a positive mindset. A positive mindset is both a powerful and an influential tool in helping us to achieve our goals. The first step in acquiring a positive mindset is making the decision to think differently and positively. As Brian Tracy puts it "If it's to be, it's up to me".

One of the ways to do this is by reading books that focus on helping you develop a positive mindset, attending seminars of influential people in the field of self-development, and listening to programs such as this, that can help you become more positive and optimistic about your life.

Another way to do this is by constantly repeating positive affirmations to ourselves, until they become a reality for us. You can also write down your affirmations 20 times daily on a piece of paper, or repeat them to yourself either out loud or silently. Do remember to ensure that they are:

- Positive
- In the present tense
- Include your name
- Specific
- And use the word 'now' and 'I' for example, "I, Jacky, am now a successful coach and mentor to many people".

The advantages to maintaining a positive mindset are many. Here are some in your work book that immediately come to my mind. There is also the opportunity to think of many more.

1. You are more enthusiastic and energetic throughout the day.

2. You tend to look on the bright side of things, rather than the gloomy side.

3. People with positive mindsets are more popular with their peers and are often an inspiration to their friends and loved ones.

4. They also tend to look at situations and problems as opportunities and are often more successful than the people who do not have a positive outlook.

5. It is a common characteristic shared by successful businessmen, entrepreneurs and other well known personalities who have achieved mastery in their lives.

MODELLING

You and I will now discuss modelling. Psychologists define behaviour modelling as a technique used to teach a child correct behaviour patterns. The technique is simple. Parents demonstrate a particular behaviour, the child copies it, the child is praised for this behaviour until it becomes a habit – this is the reason why so many of us do or say the exact same things our parents did or said. When we are children we unconsciously model our parents, it is automatic.

When you apply this technique to mastery, it is modified. You decide what it is you want to master by modelling somebody who already has the skill you desire and is successful at that skill. Instead of an external factor that influences your behaviour (i.e. parents); you choose to consciously copy or model the behaviour of others in order to achieve more in our lives. A pre-supposition of modelling is 'modelling successful performance leads to excellence'.

Modelling means to incorporate the behaviour of people, who are successful, wealthy, and accomplished into our own lives. You can do this very often both consciously and unconsciously. However the key here is to be able to identify successful behaviour and then behave the same way ourselves. Let's discuss an example: Warren Buffet is one of the most successful investors and entrepreneurs in history, and hundreds of people around the world endeavour to imitate his success both on the personal and financial front. One of the most interesting things about Warren Buffet is despite being an extremely wealthy man; he lives very frugally and also gives away up to 85% of his wealth to charity. Suppose one of my life goals is to be wealthy, I would choose to study his behaviour more closely and endeavour to be more frugal about my money in order for me to become wealthy and successful in the long term. In essence I would be modelling one of his behaviours which are not a natural behaviour pattern for me though one in which I chose to develop.

One of Mr. Buffet's other notable behaviour patterns is his absolute belief that he is wealthy, which is another behaviour that I may want to model to help me achieve my financial goals. In his own words he said "I always knew I was going to be rich. I don't think I ever doubted it for a minute."

Your workbook has an exercise on modelling which will help you identify successful people and their behaviours and also give you ideas on how to apply it to your life.

MAGENTISM

For us to now discuss magnetism I would like us for a moment for us to think about President Obama, Princess Diana, President Bill Clinton, and Mahatma Gandhi. One of the common threads running through all four of them and many other well known personalities is their absolute magnetic personalities. Their very presence radiates an incredible power for good. It is also noted that such people also generate a high degree of empathy often bringing comfort to those they come into contact with. This energy is generated from the solar plexus. This central point distributes energy to all parts of the body through the nervous system. This energy therefore creates such personal magnetism as it envelopes the body.

A magnetic personality is a person with natural charisma, self-confidence and incredible positive energy; these are people that you feel drawn to and want to be around, these are also people whose requests you do not mind fulfilling. When you or I have such a personality, we find it far easier to achieve our goals and attain mastery as we are able to influence people and achieve results in a faster and better manner.

Though there are many people who are lucky enough to be born with this magnetism, you do have the power to develop a magnetic personality as well. The exercises in your workbook will help you develop a magnetic personality.

MEDITATION

True masters believe in the power of meditation which is the topic you and I will now discuss. Many masters and coaches will tell you about the power of meditation. While many of us believe that meditation is something only monks and highly spiritual individuals do, I was pleasantly surprised to learn when I started my studies on coaching and NLP, that almost every single successful person, motivational speaker and coach uses meditation as a tool to achieve mastery. I too have learnt the tremendous benefits to be gained from meditating.

Meditation is not prayer, mediation is a deep awareness and is a state when your mind if free from all distractions and fleeting thoughts. We can think of meditation as a tool to help still your mind in order to provide you with greater clarity and a sense of calm and peace. The stillness of mind and body practised on a regular basis will help you inhibit all thoughts so that worry and fear are dissolved and replaced with only desirable thoughts. In a state of relaxation tensions are eliminated as pressure is removed from the nerves. Great freedom can be exercised as the mental faculties become relaxed. The intellect takes over and you are not controlled by the negative emotions as you allow the desirable thoughts to flow and you start to create mental pictures of the things that you desire. It is in the state of meditation that many of your answers will come to you as these come from within.

Meditation has been found to help people concentrate better, relax, have a positive effect on blood pressure, build self-confidence and a host of other mind-body benefits. Isn't Meditation a fabulous tool to help us achieve mastery?

While you can join a class or learn meditation from a book or CD, we have included a short meditation technique in your workbooks to help you get started.

Sri Chinmoy, the noted spiritual leader and Nobel Peace Prize Nominee has this advice to share on the subject of meditation. "The meditation that gives you immediate joy or continuous joy is the best meditation for you. Everyone will not have the same meditation. Your meditation will not suit me; my meditation will not suit you. You like a certain food, I don't like it. You are right in your own way I am right in my own way. But once you know what your best meditation is, please stick to it."

NEVER GIVE UP

We will now talk about how Never Give Up as an important aspect along our journey on the A-Z of Mastery program.

I include this very important aspect of Mastery. Those who never give up are the true winners in life. A Master I have chosen to learn from for internet marketing is Tom Hua who is well respected in his industry. I remember the first time I saw Tom Hua at a seminar. His message at the end of his speech was passionate to the extreme it was "Never give up, Never give up". Now this is a man who turned his life around and like all of us could have given up any time. However, he never gave up and he is living the life of his dreams tenfold and teaching others how to do the same. He realises the importance of how never giving up can transform your life. My message to you is also - never give up.

If we are able to develop this quality of never giving up, then we are able to recognize ourselves as people with special talents and abilities, and this helps us to draw on an amazing store of self-confidence despite the circumstances around and regardless of any other outside influences.

We are all plagued at times with feelings of self-doubt and even low self-confidence. Developing an attitude of never giving up can actually help us overcome these feelings and face the challenges with a positive outlook and self-confidence.

I am now going to tell you a few famous stories. I am sure you will recognize the common link between each and every one of them.

Beethoven handled the violin awkwardly and preferred playing his own compositions instead of improving his technique. His teacher called him hopeless as a composer.

Colonel Sanders had the construction of a new road put him out of business in 1967. He went to over 1,000 places trying to sell his chicken recipe before he found a buyer interested in his 11 herbs and spices. Seven years later, at the age of 75, Colonel Sanders sold his fried chicken company for a finger-lickin' $15 million!

Walt Disney was fired by a newspaper editor for lack of ideas. Disney also went bankrupt several times before he built Disneyland.

Charles Darwin, father of the theory of evolution, gave up a medical career and was told by his father, "You care for nothing but shooting, dogs, and rat catching." In his autobiography, Darwin wrote, "I was considered by my father, a very ordinary boy, rather below the common standard in intellect.

Albert Einstein did not speak until he was four years old and didn't read until he was seven. His teacher described him as "mentally slow, unsociable and adrift forever in his foolish dreams." He was expelled and refused admittance to Zurich Polytechnic School. The University of Bern turned down his Ph.D. dissertation as being irrelevant and fanciful.

George Lucas was determined. The movie Star Wars was rejected by every movie studio in Hollywood before 20th-Century Fox finally produced it. It went on to be one of the largest grossing movies in film history.

If you haven't already guessed it as yet and I am sure you have, they all have a 'Never Give Up' attitude. Despite all odds and despite what other people said about them, these individuals went on to achieve their goals and make a significant contribution to the world.

Imagine what would have happened or what would not have happened if any of them had given up on their dreams, goals and beliefs?

While ordinary people view failures and setbacks as a reason to give up, extraordinary individuals view failures and setbacks as another brief stop along the road to their success.

If you want to achieve mastery, you must develop a Never Give Up attitude, and view any obstacles in your path as nothing but minor delays and temporary setbacks, rather than a reason to throw in the towel.

More information on how to develop a Never Give Up Attitude can be found in your workbook.

OPTIMISM

You and I will now venture to talk about three more very important aspects of Mastery, those of Optimism, Originality and Omnipotent.

I read a very interesting study recently about why optimism and pessimism are both a self-fulfilling prophecy. In order to illustrate the difference between the two, I will borrow from the writings of Winston Churchill who said "A pessimist sees the difficulty in every opportunity; an optimist sees the opportunity in every difficulty."

Optimists live their lives based on the presumption that they can do something to change any situation for the better. Pessimists believe that nothing they do will make a difference to this situation.

So how does this become a self-fulfilling prophecy? If you are an optimist and are in a difficult situation, you are likely to do things to make it better which increases the chances of it becoming better, and hence fulfils that prophecy. If on the other hand you are a pessimist you are likely to do nothing which increases the chances of nothing better happening and that prophecy is fulfilled as well.

Remember we become what we think, so if you think you are an optimist, you will become one and life will be easier and more pleasant and full of opportunity for you. However if you think you are a pessimist, then you will become one and view yourself as a victim of your circumstances. Negative thinking will not produce good work. A happy optimistic mind will produce your best work. Do you think then that optimistic thoughts can produce health and prosperity? It is interesting to know that it has been proved that there is a high correlation between people who are financially successful and optimism. The majority of financial successful people are indeed optimists who were willing to look for opportunities and ways to overcome challenges and be successful. This is due to their mindset. Success is mind.

We are now going to list the top three benefits of being an optimist and four ways to turn yourself from a pessimist to an optimist. There is of course a detailed exercise on the same in your workbook.

1. Optimists achieve more

2. Optimists have better relationships with other people

3. Optimists are happier and live more fulfilled lives

Four ways to become more optimistic:

1. Exercise or meditate to release stress and tension

2. Always see the positive aspect of difficult situations

3. Think positive thoughts

4. Spend time away from negative people and enjoy the company of positive people instead, 'model' their behaviours.

ORIGINAL

Now in what way can you be original and unique. Many of us have forgotten how to be ourselves because we have spent so much of our lives being someone else. We pretend to be somebody else in order to make friends, fit in and not stand out in the crowd. In childhood and especially during our teenage years, this desire to conform was at its peak so it explains why many teenagers dress, talk and behave alike and why those that choose to be individuals are often made fun of and shunned.

It takes guts and courage to be original and I know that you are already part of that elite 1% club of people who have chosen the path of mastery and success.

As Judy Garland the famous American actress said "Always be a first-rate version of yourself, instead of a second-rate version of somebody else."

People who are brave enough to be original are also often the ones with the most ideas and the ability to think more creatively. Since you are not focussed on being someone who you are not, you are more open to new thoughts and ideas and to taking risks, which can often result in an unexpected success. Remember they thought Galileo and the theory of gravity was insanity and wanted to lock him up.

Here are some ways to be more original:

1. In order for you to be original you must first be aware of who you are and what it is that makes you – you.

2. Always think differently and creatively about problems and come up with new or alternative solutions to things.

3. Stop worrying about what people think of you

4. Believe in your individuality and look for ways to express it.

Like the American Actress Bernadette Peters said "You've gotta be original, because if you're like someone else, what do they need you for?"

OMNIPOTENT

We now move on to the word Omnipotent – and by this we mean an all powerful infinite power or the belief in our own abilities to accomplish anything that we have set out to achieve.

It is the belief that we are capable of doing anything that we set out to achieve. If you believe that you are an omnipotent or an all powerful being, then you will find no obstacles that are powerful enough to deter you from your goals and keep you from achieving mastery.

This belief is more a state of mind, and is also a self-fulfilling prophecy. The more you believe you are omnipotent, the harder you will strive to remove all obstacles from your path, the more you will achieve your goals and so this will then validate your belief in your omnipotence and motivate you to achieve more.

Some great ways and guidance on how to be optimistic, original and how to build up your belief in your own omnipotence can be found in your workbooks.

CHAPTER SIX

FROM PURPOSE TO REASON

PURPOSE

We now move onto the letter P which stands for Purpose, Passion, Potential and Philanthropic.

Living on Purpose and with Purpose and finding your life Purpose is like a glove that fits your hand. You just know when you are living with your purpose. It is an all embracing friend of yours. Without purpose there is no passion, no motivation, and no focus. When things are meaningless, you feel weak, sapped with energy. You have no enthusiasm, no joy. Everything seems trivial, empty and pointless. Getting out of bed is a chore. Have you ever felt like this? Finding your life purpose will be a revelation to you.

What is your driving force in your life right now? Is it guilt, resentment, fear, anger, need for acceptance. What would it feel like and what would it mean to you to transform this into passion, desire, joy, courage, happiness, contentment, fulfilment. Your life will have so much more meaning when you find your purpose. When you have this realisation and you really know your life purpose everything you do will move you towards leading your life purpose, no matter how small your steps are they will lead you to leading your life purpose.

You may feel that you have no idea what your life purpose is and you may feel anxious about this. You may even feel pressure. It is important for you to relax. You are not alone in this feeling. I have known several clients of mine who have felt the same. Sometimes you may have taken the wrong road. Just as when you are driving, you can turn around and go in a different direction. This is all very well, but how do you still know that your new direction is the right one for you. When you relax, just do the things that you enjoy doing. Do the things that you are drawn to. Ask yourself what do you well and truly want. Become in touch with that which you want. You will find that your life purpose has revealed itself to you at times. Examine what is coming into your life and take time to review. Ask yourself what your next step could be. Turn to your inner guidance. Often your life purpose has always been within you. Just as treasure is buried your life purpose may have been buried as other life events and influences took over your life.

I always knew deep down what my life purpose was and now through my transformational coaching aspiring others to mastery and their full potential, I really am living my life with purpose and on purpose. You can also find your life purpose for it is certainly buried within you. Let it surface and come forth. Let it come forth and unfold.

When you know your life purpose you will evaluate all your actions, activities and goals so that you drive yourself closer and closer to your life purpose. You will make rational resourceful decisions. You will become selective in all that you do for you will know what is important to you. As your life purpose unfolds ask yourself 'what can I do'? 'What is my next step'? 'How can I support my life purpose' 'what can I do to make it happen'. Be inspired by your life purpose, connect to it, manifest it daily, make it real, and write it down. Meditate and listen to your inner guidance, your intuition from within. Notice what you see. Notice what you feel – pleasure, joy, happy, content, a sense of well being, a sense of knowing. Your inner sense of well being and joy will be your compass for your life purpose. Open that treasure chest within.

In your work book this exercise will help you to reach those buried treasures you have within you.

PASSION

So now we are led to Passion. You must have passion for what you do, and more importantly you must have passion to achieve your goals and achieve mastery. Passion coach Curt Rosengren defines passion "as the energy that comes from being more of YOU into what you do". It is the love that you have for a particular task or activity that energizes you and drives you to put more of yourself into that activity.

T. Alan Armstrong the famous writer said "If there is no passion in your life, then have you really lived? Find your passion, whatever it may be. Become it, and let it become you and you will find great things happen FOR you, TO you and BECAUSE of you."

Passion is what differentiates people who love their lives and their jobs and can't wait to get up and go to work every day from people who hate their jobs and can't wait for the weekend. I encourage all my clients that if you can at this point in time, do what you love for a living and do something that you are passionate about then by all means do it.

Millions of people around the world have found that when you do something that you are passionate about, things start to happen:

1. First of all, you will love your work every day.

2. You invest more of yourself into what you do.

3. Your passion and enthusiasm is almost always noticed by your colleagues, supervisors and customers, which gets you more business and recognition.

4. You family life and personal relationships improve because you are happier and less stressful about work.

5. The chances of you becoming successful doing what you love are much higher than if you were doing something that you disliked.

Not all of us can quit our jobs and start following our dreams right this minute; however I always tell my clients that even in your current situation, you can find things about your job that you love or are passionate about. Thousands of people also choose the high road of working at their day jobs and keeping their dreams in mind by developing their passion in their own time. You may not love everything you do, however there may be aspects of your job that you enjoy, or you can talk to your boss to incorporate things that you are passionate about into your routine.

Maybe you're passionate about writing a book, or starting your own bakery. If you can't quit your day job and do that just yet, you can always write at night or bake on the weekends. The key however is to find your passion and make sure that you do something that excites you and energizes you and keeps that passion alive for you.

POTENTIAL

As a child, my teachers would often write similar comments on my end of term report cards, "A bright child with a lot of potential, however she must work hard to harness it." It was only many years later after I became a coach, that I understood the real meaning behind these words. Harness your potential now!

Each person on this planet has the potential for greatness and mastery; scientists have concluded that on an average we each use less than 10% of our total brain capacity, even Einstein, reputed to have been the most intelligent man to date only used about 15 % of his brain.

Imagine now, the potential we still have untapped within each of us. The law of attraction tells us that we are all beings with unlimited potential, and only through deliberate thought and action can we utilize this potential and achieve mastery. You become what you think you are. So if we choose to believe that we are all beings with infinite potential for greatness who can achieve anything that we put our minds to, then I am certain that we will indeed achieve everything that we set out to do.

So what stops us from achieving our potential?

- Insecurities and doubt can stop us from achieving our potential
- The fear of failure can be a barrier to us achieving our potential.
- People and events can also discourage us from achieving our potential

Anne Frank, a survivor and author of "The Diary of Anne Frank", the story of a young Jewish girl's survival during Hitler's atrocities wrote "Everyone has inside of him a piece of good news. The good news is that you don't know how great you can be! How much you can love! What you can accomplish! And what your potential is!"

Find your potential by doing the exercise in your work book.

PHILANTHROPY

Many people who have achieved greatness are also great philanthropists; they understand another law of the universe, which is the more you give of yourself in terms of time and money, the more the universe will give back to you.

Some of the noted philanthropists include Oprah Winfrey, Bill Gates, Warren Buffet, Henry Ford, Eli Lilly, W.K. Kellogg, and William Hewlett of Hewlett-Packard. As you can see, none of them showed any adverse effects from giving their wealth away. In fact in almost all these cases their wealth and fortune grew larger and larger rather than diminishing in any way.

Now while you may not be in a position to give away large amount of money to a good cause or charity, there are many other ways that you can practise philanthropy in your life. Your workbook has some great ideas on how to become a philanthropist today.

Remember as with all things, the good that you do for others will always come back to you in some way.

QUALITATIVE

Next in this program Aspiring to Mastery we will explore the concept of being qualitative. There may have been times when how much you could do or produce, took precedence over how well you did something or the quality of the product. However to achieve mastery we must be more concerned with the quality of our output versus the quantity.

Let me give you an example to help us illustrate the difference between quantity and quality: If you have children, or if you go back to the time when you were a child, what moments stick out most in your memory – the times when your parents nagged you, told you to clean your room, grounded you and a hundred other instances that you interacted with them every day, or do the times when you gathered together for a family trip, or a holiday or did something special together leap out at you and put a smile on your face. The instances which don't spring to mind immediately are the ones when as a family you spent a 'quantity' of time together however it really was not 'quality' time.

It is important for us if we want to achieve success to focus on quality and not quantity when we are working on our goals.

When working on a project it is often worth spending that extra time on it despite deadlines or your haste to get it done to ensure a quality product or result. It will always be appreciated more than a haphazard job done in less time.

When spending time with family and loved ones focus on spending quality time which creates memories and brings you closer together rather than just spending time with each other for the sake of it.

Do all that you can to bring quality into every aspect of your life. I learned early on in the value of buying 'quality' clothes over 'quantity' clothes. If you can only buy one coat or business suit, buy the best that you can afford at the time. When I have done this, I find that I can wear that outfit for some time without it showing any signs of wear. The clothes that I pick up just because they were less expensive or half price, are often never worn, thrown out or given away after a season.

Developing a qualitative mindset also means focussing on the quality of stimulus that you feed your mind. Rather than watching six hours of television for example, you may want to watch one show that makes you laugh, or inspires you. Look at the books, magazines, newspapers and music that you listen to? Are they quality items, or is it just quantity that you are feeding yourself? I used to buy multiple magazines and journals to read; now I spend time only on the ones I really enjoy and that enrich my life.

You can also apply this concept to food and drink. The French are only too happy to extol the virtues of quality over quantity in regards to gastronomy. This is perhaps the reason why they apparently spend the most money per household on groceries than the rest of the world.

In personal relationships too, it is not the number of people that you know that matter. It is the quality of the relationships that you have with them. You may be an extremely sociable person, like I am, however when we really think about it, there are those extra special friends in which you know you can rely and count upon. You chose your friends for the qualities that they bring into your life, the values they have, the special moments that you spend with them. They are an extension of your joy and happiness. Choose your friends with the same care that you chose expensive clothes – pick quality over quantity.

As Aristotle the ancient Greek Philosopher, Scientist and Physician said "Quality is not an act, it is a habit".

QUICK WITTED

Q is also for Quick Witted and by this we mean quick to understand a situation and quick to act. People, who have achieved greatness in their lives, have always had the ability to quickly grasp a situation and act accordingly. With the ability to grasp a situation, rationalise and reason, always thinking of the consequences of action, generates a greater understanding which is needed for Mastery. Though many people are naturally quick witted if you think you are not, fear not it is a skill that can be learnt and developed.

Learning to be quick witted is simply a matter of expanding your knowledge, learning to think faster and more clearly and also being able to focus on the situation and understand it better.

There are more ideas on how to incorporate quality into your life and how to develop your ability to be quick witted in your workbook.

RESPONSILBITY

The 3 R's stand for Responsibility, Rigour and Reason.

What do we mean by responsibility? It is taking complete responsibility for ourselves, our actions and even our thoughts.

Remember the law of attraction teaches us that our lives are a direct manifestation of our thoughts and the things that they attract into our lives. Therefore in order for us to be happy and successful we must first accept responsibility for the fact that we ourselves are responsible for our own thoughts and hence we are responsible for the things that are manifesting themselves into our lives.

When we talk about accepting responsibility this is what it means:

- Acknowledging the fact that you and only you are responsible for the choices that you make in your life.
- Accepting that you are responsible for what YOU CHOOSE to feel and think
- Accepting that you chose the direction that your life will take
- Accepting that you cannot blame others for your choices and bad decisions or circumstances

- Accepting that how you feel about something is entirely up to you.
- Taking responsibility for your health and well-being
- Taking the ownership of being your own cheerleader, writing your own affirmations and forming your own motivating thoughts.

When you fail to take responsibility for your actions it is easy to become negative or blame people that you think have affected your life; you become overly dependent on other people; you tend to neglect your emotional and physical well-being; you become fearful of failure and criticism and other behaviours that will not allow you to become successful or achieve your goals and dreams.

Some ways to accept responsibility include:

- Realizing that everything we do has a consequence
- Stop looking for ways to assign blame, look for solutions instead
- Forgive yourself
- Think positive thoughts and shun bad ones

These following words are so true "My philosophy is that not only are you responsible for your life, but doing the best at this moment puts you in the best place for the next moment," as quoted by Oprah Winfrey. This is clearly telling you that by accepting responsibility now, you will be far better equipped to move forward.

The exercises in your work book will help you with responsibility.

RIGOUR

In order to achieve the goals that we have set for ourselves we must make rigour a part of our mastery arsenal. Rigour simply means to do something consistently over a period of time in order to achieve results.

I am sure that you can relate to this, there are times when you are probably turbo-charged at the beginning of each year, brimming with goals and resolutions and action plans. Somewhere between the 1st and the 3rd quarter, intentions seem to faze out and lose their intensity. When October rolls around however, you find yourself motivated again and scrambling to achieve as much as possible in what's left of the year.

If you had maintained the rigour that you had initially when the year had started, you would have been able to accomplish a lot more of your goals in perhaps a shorter time. That is the power of rigour, a consistent and focussed effort throughout the entire duration of a project and not just in the beginning and the end.

REASON

The last R stands for Reason, we've already discussed how motivation can be both external and internal and that internal motivation is often stronger and more powerful than external motivation. One of the ways to effectively motivate yourself to do something from within is to identify the reason that you are doing it in the first place.

If you have a good solid reason for doing the things that need doing, it is often much easier to actually take action. Have you ever suddenly asked yourself why you are doing something? You need to know your reason WHY with whatever you do in life.

Let's take for instance the example of someone who is overweight and has been that way all their lives. They go for their annual medical check-up and their doctor informs them of all the health-risks associated with being over-weight, suddenly you find them eating healthier and exercising, all because they have a REASON to get fitter and healthier.

The same way if you are a parent or in a leadership position at work, you will find it much easier to get people to do what you want them to do if you give them the reasons behind your request.

Rather than asking an employee to work late on a Friday night, it is far more effective to give him your reasons for asking him to give up part of his weekend and stay and work for you. He may still not be happy about your request; however he will understand

SOLUTIONS

When a problem arises have you ever found yourself focusing on the following:

1. What caused the problem

2. The problem itself

3. Who caused the problem and hence who is to blame

4. The consequences of the problem

What you need to do instead is focus on finding a solution to the problem, 'Instead of crying over spilt milk; you may want to look for a mop to clean up the mess instead'.

On our journey to mastery, it is worthwhile to develop a solution-orientation to problems. Solution-orientated thinking may seem hard at first; however like most things it becomes easier with time and practice. So the next time you face a problem or a difficult situation, you need to consciously tell yourself to STOP focussing on the problem and start focussing on finding a solution instead. There is without doubt always a solution to every single problem however complex or simple it may appear to be. The problem that you cannot solve does not exist.

Look within and when looking for a solution remember to ask questions that begin with What, and How versus Why, When or Who. Focus on what 'you' can do, versus 'them', 'they', 'we' or 'you'. You can know and do just exactly what is necessary to solve the issue. Your solution should always be centred on action.

STRATEGY

Another word beginning with S to use in this program is Strategy. I am sure the CEO of any company will tell you it is absolutely vital to have a sound strategy in place for the company to be successful. An organisations aims and objectives are often described in a business plan. Most often a company when they are placing strategies, they will reorganise and restructure in order to increase their return on investments and profitability. We also have personal strategies where we can have a return on the energies in which we place; these can be mental, physical or spiritual. A strategy is always going to be a sequence of thoughts in which we use in order to think and plan our actions to achieve our outcomes. Strategies are the key ways in which we either do or do not achieve our desired outcome. Our internal processing strategies control our external behaviours. It is important that the desired outcome has a defined sensory representation. You need to have belief that the outcome is worth doing, you can do it, and you deserve to do it. All strategies that are successful will use specific language and words that will stimulate the senses – the vision, the feeling, the sound, the taste, the smell. A strategy is essentially a plan with clear cut objectives that you want to achieve, and goals that you which to accomplish.

You have a strategy in place for almost everything that you do in life from getting up in the morning to everything else that you do. Once you have a strategy, how do you know it is the best strategy? Running through it several times and examining it to see if anything needs changing is one way of changing a strategy. In NLP there is a model called the TOTE model which is used in order to test a strategy. TOTE stands for Test, Operate, Test, Exit. It is a model for becoming more efficient at what you do.

More information on Strategy can be found in your work book.

SYSTEMS

Another useful business and personal practice to follow is to have systems in place for tasks that you do routinely and on a frequent basis or are essential for running your business and daily life. Essentially systems are processes that exist to ensure that work is carried out in a prescribed manner. An example of this is a system for sorting your incoming mail, many of us; myself included get tons of junk mail every day. Some time ago, I would end up missing my bills, and binned important mail simply because I did not have a proper system in place. Now I open each envelope as it comes in, and I either bin it, put it in the 'to respond', 'to file' or 'to pay' trays on my desk. This system helps me to stay on top of all my mail all the time.

In systems we also need to look at those systems which become efficient repeatable actions in order for us to fulfil our goals in the most effective way possible. This may be automation, service standards, performance evaluation, and time keeping. Efficient and repeatable systems will ensure that the plan is executed with greater efficiency. One minute spent on planning can save ten or more minutes in execution. Think of the return on your personal investment in terms of it being tenfold. Systems and planning are worth every single minute of your time. Start to plan now.

SPIRIT

Together we will now explore Spirit. While the word spirit has many different meanings, we mean that to achieve mastery one must also have spirit or a vital or animating force that comes from within you. We often refer to people around the holidays as having Christmas Spirit or being filled with holiday cheer and energy. In the same way we must strive to be infused with this same spirit and energy at all times. To be infused with spirit is to live with vitality and energy, enthusiasm and confidence which you share with others. It is often referred to as the spirit into which we enter into something. It is this spirit which we must strive for continuously. Living with true spirit will raise your level of consciousness in all areas of your life so that you are living in a spirit and consciousness of more happiness, health, wealth, power. When you live within the spirit of such things, they will naturally be a part of you and yours by a right. When we recognise our spiritual nature our accomplishments increase as enthusiasm, desire, courage and faith are developed further.

Being a person of Spirit, can help us face each day with more energy and enthusiasm and make our personal and work relationships stronger and more meaningful.

STRENGTH

A vital key in this program is Strength. The path to mastery and achieving our goals may not be an easy one and we will face many obstacles and setbacks along the way. Any thoughts of lack, limitation, fear, or distress will produce exactly that. The only way to overcome these disappointments and setbacks is to develop our inner strength which allows us to remain strong, focussed and positive despite all adversity. Out of effort emerges strength. The extent to which we apply effort to overcome such adversities and obstacles will manifest itself in strength proportionality. Develop a permanent inner strength. It is through your objective mind that you will develop an inner strength. Correct thinking will send constructive feelings through your nervous system and in turn your inner strength will be constructed.

As Mariah Carey the noted American pop singer said "You really have to look inside yourself and find your own inner strength, and say, "I'm proud of what I am and who I am, and I'm just going to be myself.""

For more ideas on how to implement systems in your daily life and how to find and develop your inner strength use the exercises in your work book.

SERVICE

A really important factor that we shall now look at is Service. Now if you really are very serious about attracting wealth and success into your life you will need to focus on an idea of how you can be of Service to others. I have already mentioned that your riches are within you and this starts with an idea. How can you help people; how can you be of a service to them; how can you give greater value; how can you help them to make money? Giving a service will mean that you too will benefit. If you are employed, think of more ways that you can be of a service to your employer in order that they reward you with remuneration and promotion. How can you help and be of service to your peers, customers, your boss, stakeholders, and systems. How can you be of service to everybody that you come into contact with? Does it not equate that the more value and service that you give, the more you will be rewarded? Your very intentions will be based upon some core principles and laws of fairness and integrity in order for this to work. Find out what people need, how you can be of service to them and supply this service to them with fairness and integrity.

There are of course some exercises in your workbook on Service.

TENACITY

The letter T stands for Tenacity, Thought and Truth.

The dictionary defines Tenacity as persistence in maintaining or seeking something valued or desired. We can also define tenacity to mean the courage and persistence to repeat something over and over again, or to stick to a routine or schedule in order to achieve mastery.

You will recall earlier in the book we spoke about the power of Meditation in helping us achieve mastery. Like so many things we wish to master, in order to learn and master the art of meditation, we have to practice it diligently every day. In other words we have to be tenacious in our desire to learn meditation.

Much about the road to mastery is about learning new habits and keeping to them. It is learning to let go of old and unrewarding patterns of behaviour in order to learn new ones that are more rewarding for us.

Learning to be tenacious is one such rewarding habit. We have heard it said over and over again that it took Thomas Edison thousands of attempts before he finally produced the light bulb. However there are countless famous examples of people who were persistent and tenacious despite all the odds.

If you want to be more tenacious in your life you must:

- Give everything you have to the cause
- Work with determination and not wait for things to happen, in other words to take charge of your life.
- Quit only once the job is over and not when you feel tired, fed up or possibly defeated by it.

Let's think back on our lives for a moment. Are there situations in your life when you wish you had given it one more attempt, or experimented a little harder in order to achieve something you really wanted? Did you ever quit before you got what you wanted and wished you hadn't done that?

I can think of at least three instances in my life when I wish I had been more tenacious! Now think of your life right now. Is there a problem or situation in your life right now in which you think you should be more tenacious in order to get what you want? There is more than one in my life and I am sure there is at least one situation in yours too. Think what the rewards would be if you applied the principle of tenacity to that situation.

THOUGHT

Thought is powerful which is what you and I shall now discuss. IBM's founder Thomas J Watson Senior once said that "All the problems of the world could be settled easily if men were only willing to think. The trouble is that men very often resort to all sorts of devices in order not to think, because thinking is such hard work."

Do you not think therefore that the ability to think is a trait which is valued in all successful people and is vital for you and I if we want to achieve mastery in our lives. Now I know your thinking, 'Jacky – we already know how to think', and I agree with you. However, here we are more interested in the power of a thought and the impact that it can have on our lives, as opposed to the mechanism of how to form a thought. We learnt in the movie The Secret that thoughts have power and that thoughts become things. Therefore a single thought repeated over and over either silently or out loud has the power to change our lives from what it currently is to what we wish for it to be.

Many of us forget or do not acknowledge the power of our thoughts. It has already been mentioned that we have more than 70,000 thoughts a day. Many of these thoughts are the same thoughts we had yesterday and will have again tomorrow. What do you really want to be thinking so that your thoughts will create a better life for you starting right now? Do you know that you can consciously change the thought you are having by simply repeating an affirmation over and over again to yourself? I never realised this until I did this myself one day and it was true. Now for instance, repeat the words 'I am wealthy' over and over again to yourself all day long. Is it that hard to do? Imagine if you repeat this thought to yourself for a week, a month, a year; imagine the power that this thought will generate to turn you into a person of wealth. And really believe it. Remember as we believe – so will we receive. Anything in which we hold continuously and for a length of time in our subconscious mind will make an impression upon it and through this we create our own experiences which are attracted to us from the world without. So everything from without is attracted to us from our world within. Your thoughts are like magnets. Your predominant thought is a strong magnet which will form your personality from your mental attitude. Positive constructive thoughts should create good and harmony in your life. They will take root. Thoughts which are from positive qualities such as determination, courage, faith, kindness, inspiration. In fact any of the qualities in which we are discussing in this program Aspiring To Mastery will be evident in your environment, your heath, wealth, and happiness. Is this not all that you wish for! Everything that happens in your life starts with a thought. There is only thought. This is a powerful connection and realisation. Immerse yourself with quality thoughts right now!

TRUTHFUL

The last T is perhaps one of the hardest and most courageous habits for us to master. It is the ability to be truthful. When we talk about the truth, we do not mean only telling the truth when asked; we also mean being true to ourselves and our values 100% of the time. I was reading a speech by an evangelical leader recently and he said something very interesting – he said that in the bible 'integrity is not a gift, unlike many other spiritual gifts; integrity is something god wants you to work out on your own.' I would like to share with you the following three aspects to the truth and living a life of truthfulness:

1. To live truthfully – your thoughts must match your actions and vice versa.

2. Be true to your thinking – your thoughts must not be corrupted by deceit or self-deception.

3. Speak and act truthfully - there must be a correlation between what you say you will do and what you actually do.

Now you and I know that to be truthful to ourselves and all who we deal with in life is the ideal that we all strive towards.

Some examples of situations when it is absolutely vital that we speak the truth are:

1. We must tell the truth when people have the right to know the truth. Like when selling someone a new service or product.

2. Second, we must tell the truth with the relationships we are in be it our spouse, business partner, clients customers etc.

3. Thirdly – we must tell the truth to people if their well-being depends on that truth.

Here are some situations when it is considered correct to withhold information and this is when you are being true unto others. For instance:

1. When the truth would result in violence to others.

2. If the truth violates a confidence of someone else for instance when I am coaching I am honour bound to hold my clients secrets in the strictest confidence.

3. If I have promised not to tell a secret, then I have the right to withhold it from a third person.

4. If telling the truth violates my privacy in some way then I have the right to withhold the truth.

If our actions are not in harmony with the truth then confusion and discord will be the result. Discord and confusion will disappear when congruency of truth is applied. There is great satisfaction when you stand confidently in your truth. Truth is the very foundation from which every personal and business relationship is built upon. When we know the truth we are able to apply constructive, accurate and correct thinking. The principle of truth will precede every right action. The truth indeed will set you free.

More ideas and exercises on Tenacity, Thought and Truth can be found in your workbook.

CHAPTER SEVEN

FROM UNIVERAL MIND TO ZEAL

UNIVERAL MIND

In this part of the program we will be covering the Universal Mind and also the quality of being Unstoppable.

Now let us recall the part of Chapter one where we discussed the conscious mind and the subconscious mind. The conscious mind being the gatekeeper of the sub conscious mind. The sub conscious mind being the loyal obedient servant of the conscious mind. The sub-conscious mind being the store house of every single thought and belief that we have. Those who achieve mastery make use of the third mind - the universal mind and learn how to develop this.

The mind in essence is what makes us human beings and what makes us special. Without the mind we would not be aware that we existed, and hence we would not exist. Despite all our differences, our lifestyles and the advances made in science, all human beings have the same questions that they want answered in their lives. Why am I here? What is the purpose of my life? Where did we come from? So it stands to reason that if we take away all the things that make us individuals, we are all essentially united by a common bond or thread. We all have the same needs and we all seek answers to the same questions. It stands to reason then that we are interconnected in some way and we are all a part of a larger consciousness whether we are aware of this or not. We call this consciousness the universal mind. The connection to this though comes from within.

In this way we believe that the universe is filled with energy and vibrations that are open to anyone who wishes to connect with and tap into. It is said that psychic people know about this energy because they have taught themselves to focus on and connect into this energy in order to derive answers.

The steps to tapping into the universal consciousness are:

1. Learning to focus on this energy and becoming conscious of it

2. Understanding that every single living thing on this planet is connected to every other thing.

3. Practice mind exercises and techniques designed to help you tap into this consciousness.

4. Meditation is a key tool used to tap into the universal mind

When you are able to connect into this storehouse of cosmic energy and power, you are able to connect with and draw energy from every other living being in the universe. If you train your mind to tap into this power then you have an infinite well of energy and potential at your disposal when you want and need it.

Often when many great teachers of the law of attraction tell you to inform the universe of your desire, let it go and allow the universe to fulfil this desire, they are talking about projecting your desire to this shared universal mind, and letting that shared consciousness manifest your desire for you. So you see why it is so important for us to understand the concept of the universal mind and also learn how to tap into it. This universal fountain of supply is powered from your world within you as you are the outlet for this energy. When we fully use the creative power of thought and act as though all that we desire has already been achieved then this will be the impression made upon the universal mind. Your mental images and ideals formed by this creativity will be received by this power and the consequence is that these causes are set into motion. The universal mind has unlimited resourcefulness and we are the very manifestation of that mind. As we now have an understanding in this program Aspiring to Mastery of how the conscious mind, the sub conscious mind and the universal mind operates it becomes more and more apparent how important it is that we look after the gate keeper of our subconscious and universal minds in order for us to connect and create all that we desire in life. As we connect and unite to the universal mind we become less conscious of any limitations and more conscious of the unconditional universal mind. This leads to our empowerment, creativity, the realisation of our own power from within and infinite unlimited potential. Drawing on the power within creates greater possibilities This is when we truly do become free and masters of our own destiny for we will have found the source of all that is good and all that we seek.

UNSTOPPABLE

Another key to mastery is the belief that you are Unstoppable! Throughout this program we have talked about the power of our thoughts, and how we become everything that we believe and our potential to manifest the things that we believe in. One of the things that we MUST believe in is our own ability to be unstoppable!

Now does this sound familiar to you? I know this has happened to me in the past. We make up our minds to achieve a new goal or begin a new project and jump in with guns ablaze ready to face all the challenges that life could hurl at us. Inevitably the challenges did come, and perhaps people around us were less than supportive, we became busy, we lost focus, other life events took over, and then a few weeks or months down the line we gave up on the project and most importantly ourselves. We stopped believing in ourselves and in our ability to be unstoppable and we gave in to the belief that we could be defeated.

The great masters across the ages never believed that they were anything other than unstoppable beings, destined for success and greatness. Mahatma Gandhi believed he was unstoppable, so did Nelson Mandela, so did Walt Disney, so did Henry Ford, so did Oprah Winfrey. Each and every one of these individuals believed at the core of their being that their goals and missions were important and critical enough that nothing and no one could stop them from achieving what they set out to do.

When you learn how to become unstoppable you too will become a dynamic force, and anyone or anything that crosses your path will get swept up in your enthusiasm and energy.

There are some great exercises in your workbook to help you tap into universal consciousness and how to be unstoppable.

VALUES

To achieve mastery in our lives we must have Values, Vision, Vibration and Vitality or the 4 V's in our lives. If we recall, personal mastery is a journey towards continuous improvement and this journey is guided with the key principles of values vision, vibration, and vitality.

Do you ever wonder why at times you have set a goal with every intention of fulfilling it and yet you just cannot find the motivation to really set upon its accomplishment? Somehow you feel unfulfilled and empty. I know that this has happened to me in the past. This is where we must look to our values, for every goal and vision must be congruent and in alignment with our values in order for it to really mean something to us and therefore lead us to taking the appropriate actions. If we are unclear about our values we will not be making clear objective decisions in our lives. How can we take the appropriate actions if we are not making clear objective decisions? We need to know our values and truly own them. We need to know what we really want from anything in our life. What values do you want in the end? What really matters to you? When every decision you make is related to your very own personal core values you no matter what will live by those values. Your values are at the very essence of your character.

Some of your core values which motivate you towards a highly motivated state have already been mentioned in this program Aspiring To Mastery. For instance they may be Determination, Focus, Love, Harmony, Truth, and Health. There are other values which will truly motivate you such as Freedom, Comfort, and Adventure. Your values may not all have equal importance to you; some will rank higher than others. Knowing or even changing your values can really change your life for you will consistently live with true purpose and meaning.

There is a great exercise on Values in your workbook to help you really work on your values.

VISION

If mastery is a journey that all of us have made a commitment to embark on, then vision is like the compass that keeps us from straying too far from our path.

A vision is a powerful force that will change your life. Most organizations have a vision statement from which they set their short term, medium term and long term goals so that they are in alignment. In the same way it is possible for us as individuals to develop personal vision statements which help guide our decisions and influence our choices on a daily basis.

A vision statement is often the first step to focussing your life and can be the single most important thing that you can do to fill your life with success and achievement. Your personal vision statement takes into account the things that you enjoy doing every day, the aspects of your work that you enjoy, your values, and your life goals across different areas of your life.

Unlike our goals and desires, a personal vision statement rarely changes. It is something that we propel ourselves towards. It guides our decisions and is often a reason for our existence. So you can see why it is so important for us to have a vision statement in hand when we begin our journey to mastery. Creating a vision statement that is all encompassing and comprehensive can be enlightening.

Another way to create your vision is to use a vision board. A vision board is an extension of your vision statement in pictorial form. To create your vision board, place pictures of your life goals and dreams onto a cork or similar board and put it somewhere that you can look at it every day. It is your perfect picture of how you want your life to be. Your life images need to surround you. They need to be all that you want and desire. Look at you vision board and say "all this is mine NOW". Become emotionally involved with your vision. Feel the joy, the pleasure, the excitement, the bliss, the passion, the happiness.

Many success coaches myself included believe that a vision board is one of the most powerful tools you can use to achieve your goals; it is much easier for our sub-conscious to process pictures and words as opposed to written statements. I have used this vision board exercise when coaching Chief Executive Officers on their company vision. I remember one CEO who was very sceptical and I asked that he trust in the process. He now uses this method all the time to create the vision for his company.

When you make mental images your future will emerge from the visualisation. Place no limitation upon that which you desire. Use your imagination. Be as creative as possible. Your ideal must be created, not a detail to be left out. Know what your harvest is. In the words of Dr Stephen Covey the Author of The Seven Habits Of Highly Effective People "Begin with the end in mind" . Know exactly what it is that you want in every detail. Use the process of meditation until you have absolute clarity on the vision. Visualisation will create the detail as little by little it starts to emerge and unfold. If you are for instance visualising your dream home, visualise it exactly how you want it to be, every room, every window, door, furnishings, colour schemes, location, price, size of the grounds in every detail. Do not leave anything out. Reach your ideal.

Be definite. Be specific. Repeatedly have this image in mind so that the image is strongly planted in your mind so that every cell in your body can work upon attracting your ideal to you. Affirm that you already have your ideal. With constant repetition, powerful affirmations and mental images, your ideal will become part of you.

VIBRATION

This now leads us onto talking about vibration. The Secret and other books on the Law of Attraction are filled with advice on how to raise your vibration. To attract something into your life you must raise your vibration to match that of the person or object that you desire. Negative vibrations are associated with negative feelings like anger, fear and resentment while positive and higher vibrations are associated with positive feelings like love, peace and balance. Our vibration attracts to us things which are at the same frequency as us and people with the same vibrational frequency as us. Hence there is much truth to the saying 'like attracts like'.

So the next time you want to manifest something in your life or focus on manifesting something into your life, remember to first check the vibrations that you are giving out. Remember that raising your vibration also fills you with energy and enthusiasm and hence is a two-fold effect. Our thoughts will raise our vibration and vibration will be determined by the frequency and amplitude. The higher the rate of vibration is in itself the ability of the individual to be in tune with the source of all life. For vibration is life. A positive and high vibration will raise your consciousness of life. A life of truth is the highest possible vibration.

Here are some of my favourite ways to raise my vibration:

- Listen to an upbeat song
- Watch comedy shows
- Watch a funny movie
- Write in a gratitude journal
- Go for a walk in nature
- Exercise

- Do something nice for someone
- Play with a pet
- Clean and de-clutter
- Live in vibrational congruence with that which you desire
- Read or listen to something motivational – yes this CD means right now by the very act of listening to it and carrying out the exercises, you are raising your vibration.

There are many other ways to raise your vibration some teachers of the law of attraction have numerous processes designed to help you raise your vibration. However in my experience, if it makes you feel happy, joyous, and congruent then it's probably a simple effective way to get you to the right vibration to manifest the things you want out of your life.

VITALITY

The last V stands for Vitality. Vitality means more than one thing. Vitality first and foremost means energy. Since everything in this universe is made up of varying amounts of energy, and energy is what attracts things and people to us, it stands to reason that the more energetic we are and the more vitality we have, the more we will be able to manifest in our lives. If we lead healthy and energetic lives, we are also able to achieve mastery in a faster and more effective way. Vitality is more than physical energy; it is that undeniable spark which lights up your life and the lives of those around you. To be filled with vitality is to be energetic both spiritually and physically and to live your life with an incredible energy and enthusiasm.

In order to live a healthy lifestyle full of vitality and energy, here are some techniques to incorporate into your life and day.

1. Eat foods that make you feel more energetic and healthy.

2. Do enough exercise, enough to make you full of energy and not so much as to drain you.

3. Balance your work/social and me time so that you give enough time to each aspect of your life.

4. Visualize your vitality and set a goal on a scale of 1 to 10 of how vital you want to be and what you think your current level of vitality is.

Your workbooks have more ideas on how you can lead a healthier, energetic and more vital life, which will allow you to attract more of what you want into your life.

WILL

The letter W stands for Will, Wisdom and Wealth.

Christopher Reeve the actor who played Superman had this to say on the subject of Will "So many of our DREAMS at first seem Impossible, then they seem Improbable, and then when we Summon the Will, they soon become Inevitable."

In order to continue on our journey to mastery and continuous improvement we need to have incredible will or will power. Willpower can also be defined as the art of replacing one habit for another. During the course of this program we have talked about many habits that we must incorporate into our lives or replace our old habits with. This is why will is such an integral part of mastery. When we place all our attention on something and concentrate 100%, it is the power of our will that is directing us. When we have experienced success, joy, happiness, again it is natural for us to place our attention on the positive effects of these experiences. This will motivate us and by our will we will create more of this into our life.

While belief is what fuels our actions, will is what brings inner strength, self mastery and decisiveness. Will is our inner ability to overcome excuses, laziness, and procrastination. It is our innate ability to make a decision and stick with it despite how difficult it seems.

Every single person who has achieved greatness in life has had immense reservoirs of will power to rely on to help see them through. One of the most influential stories about Will and the persistence to see things through is that of Abraham Lincoln the 16th President of the United State. He started life in a one room log cabin in Kentucky. He faced countless defeats during his life, lost eight elections, failed in business multiple times over, and suffered a nervous breakdown. However despite all this, he still had the will to go on to win the presidency of the United States. He was instrumental in the abolishment of slavery and is considered one of the most influential men in history today.

WISDOM

The next W you and I will now look at Wisdom. Wisdom is different from knowledge and it has nothing to do with age. Even young children are capable of being wise and more senior individuals may not possess this trait. Wisdom is the ability to think of the consequences of our actions and desires and then acting accordingly. Cultivating the habit of wisdom allows us to make wise and sound judgements. It also helps us to gain a reputation for providing wise judgements to our peers and loved ones who will start to come to us for advice. While some people seem to be born infinitely wise, don't despair if you are not one of them, you can still cultivate wisdom in your life.

Oprah Winfrey has this advice to share about cultivating wisdom "Follow your instincts. That's where true wisdom manifests itself."

Socrates the Greek philosopher is considered to have been the wisest man who ever lived, yet he never wrote any books and most of his wisdom was through advice that has been passed on till present day. Much of his advice, was a result of much thought and deliberation, and hence seemed to others as wise and philosophical advice.

Some of his pearls that have been passed down to us till today include advice like this: "To find yourself, think for yourself." And "True knowledge exists in knowing that you know nothing. And in knowing that you know nothing, that makes you the smartest of all."

Those who recognise the power of thought are wise and understand that in this they are the masters of their own destiny.

Here are some ways for us to cultivate the habit of wisdom in our lives:

- Associate with wise people
- Don't jump to conclusions
- When making decisions, seek the wisdom of wise and learned people
- Realize and admit that you don't know it all
- Don't make decisions without gathering complete information
- Do all you can to understand the reason and intent behind an action
- Read and apply what you read
- Do not be judgemental

For more exercises on both will and wisdom turn to your workbooks when you are ready.

WEALTH

The last W stands for Wealth and is a word that almost all of us would like to be associated with. Wealth is essentially the resources that you presently own and your ability to use these resources in such a way that you are able to do the things you want to do and when you want to do them. Wealth is more a feeling of abundance, and it means different things to different people. Wealth is relative. The amount of money that I have in the bank may make me feel like a wealthy person, whereas the same amount of money could be insufficient for you. The original meaning of the word wealth means 'the condition of well being'. Genuine wealth then is not merely a function of how much money you have in the bank, or your assets. Genuine wealth is the condition of well being in all aspects of your life, namely:

- Personal
- Professional
- Spiritual
- Environmental
- Financial

However in our lives, being financially wealthy is a large concern for many of us. Now think of this for a moment. Everything has an exchange value. The most predominant characteristic of wealth is its exchange value. This exchange value will need to satisfy our ideals and will therefore be a means to accomplishing our ideals and desires. It is this ideal in which we strive for, a definite fixed purpose. In order to reach your ideal it is essential that you recognise opportunities, to keep an open mind, and reach for new things. Ask yourself how these opportunities can help you to help other people make money so that they too can benefit, for this will turn out to be your best success. The true masters of Wealth are those that made money for other people as in the case of Rockefeller and Carnegie. All wealth as mentioned already in this program starts with an idea. That idea starts with a thought. That thought is within you. Wealth is therefore within you. This is a revelation in itself. Imagine your wealth within you.

In your workbooks you will find an exercise that describes the following steps to becoming wealthy one small step at a time.

1. Step 1 – changing the way we think about money

2. Step 2 – Understanding the power of small amounts

3. Step 3 – Savings = Freedom

4. Step 4 – your life is your responsibility

5. Step 5 – buy the stock not the product

6. Step 6 – invest in yourself first

7. Step 7 – Money is not an answer

8. Step 8 – create new ways than those taught to you by your parents

9. Step 9 – stop worrying

10. Step 10 – how can you benefit others

Using these tips and ideas should set you off on your path to financial freedom and wealth in no time. Remember that true mastery is about continuous improvement in all aspects of our lives, including our financial lives.

X-FACTOR

The X factor is a certain indefinable quality that makes certain people stand out from others. The X factor in interviews is often what makes a certain candidate stand out from the rest; in acting the X factor is what lands a potential actress a certain part despite other actresses being prettier or sexier than her. The X factor is what makes actresses like Whoopi Goldberg and Julie Walters, both not conventional actresses, stand out from the crowd and land wonderful parts. It is not very easy to define what makes up the X factor for different people, and it's often the hardest thing to place your finger on – most people will describe it as 'that certain something' that somebody has about them.

We like to think that the X factor is that Extra factor that you add to your personality. It is what allows us to stand out from the crowd and makes people stand up and take notice of us.

Although no two people have the same kind of X factor, there are some common attributes; the first being confidence, people with the X factor have extremely high levels of self-confidence. And of course they truly believe in themselves.

They are also aware of what makes them different. In order for you to stand out from the crowd you must first know what it is that makes you stand out in the first place. Instead of hiding the things that make them different, these people celebrate their differences and often flaunt them. It is their unconditional acceptance, self-confidence and love for themselves which leads to that certain attribute that we call the X-factor.

Cindy Crawford instead of covering her mole, made it her trademark and it went to become one of the recognized moles in modelling history. Oprah Winfrey, embraced the things that made her different and went on to become one of the most celebrated talk show hosts in television history.

Let's take a moment here and list 3 people in your life, either people you know personally or people who are famous who you think have that X factor. What is this X factor that they have? What are the attributes that make you feel that they posses this X factor – list them down? What can you do to incorporate the X factor into your personality?

Here are some more ways to find your X factor:

- Do things that make you stand out from the crowd or that express your individuality.
- Be aware of your strengths, and of the things that make you unique and special.
- Have courage to shine or stand out in a crowd.
- Love yourself and work on your confidence.
- Be enthusiastic and learn to embrace life and the challenges that it throws your way.

YEN

We shall now discuss the power of Yen – to have a strong desire. Every one of us has wishes and hopes for the future; however this is not enough for the true master; the true master has a strong and unquenchable burning desire to achieve his goals and desires. They place all their desires and energies into manifesting what it is that they really want from their lives. They also have a definite purpose and ambition and are crystal clear about what they want to achieve in their lives.

If you wish to attain mastery and achieve your goals you must have the following:

1. A clear specific vision of what you want

2. A relentless burning desire to achieve this vision

3. Be able to see yourself achieving your goals. Notice what you see, feel and hear when visualising your goals

4. Be able to imagine your goals in such clarity that the goal seems very real until it manifests itself into your life.

5. True masters also never accept defeat. Believe in your dreams despite obstacles and setbacks.

When a master really identifies with his desire and all concentration is impressed upon it he will be so engrossed in the thought that his mind becomes a magnet. Through this he develops that real burning strong desire which is planted into the sub conscious mind. Whatever their ideal is in health, wealth and happiness, they actually see it and believe it. They have full knowledge of what they want, and to possess it all starts with that strong desire. There is more on Yen in your workbook.

ZEN

The last letter of the alphabet and our program is Z and we have the three Z's of Zen, Zest and Zeal to talk about.

Zen is a Japanese word which means many things. Basically the word Zen means meditation, though many people use the word in other context, it essentially is a way to meditate in Japanese culture. Zen is not a religion, though there is a form of Zen Buddhism, nor is it specific to any culture in particular. It is something that each and every one of us can benefit from as we embark on our road to mastery. Zen is also a way of living your life and relating the principles to your daily life. If you decorate your room keeping in mind the principles of Zen for example, it simply means that your room is a restful and tranquil place that is capable of drawing you into a state of meditation.

Joseph Campbell, who we've heard from before, the American mythologist and writer, said of Zen practice is like an athlete when he's in the zone, except all of the time.' I thought it would be great to live and handle challenges and interact with people like I was in that zone all of the time. Don't you?

While it takes time and practice to incorporate Zen techniques into your life, here are some ways that we can all add a little Zen to our days. Zen teaches focus, concentration and self-control.

- Practice focussed breathing techniques

- Approach everything with a clean and fresh mind

- Practice mindfulness or the awareness of things that go on outside us and within us as well

Zen is also about our approach to the way we live, and work. Living with Zen also means to have a clean peaceful home and a well organized neat work space. It stands to reason that a clean and well organized space help us to think more clearly and focus better on our day to day activities.

It is said that great minds seek solitude and silence. Zen is very much the ability to look within ourselves. Our world within is related to our subconscious mind and consists of our power, thoughts and feelings which is all within our control. From our world within is the answer to every single problem or issue. Look within and we shall find the answer. There is no need to search without. Everything lies within you. I believe that intuition is our tuition from within. Take heed of this tuition for it is your guide and will always lead you to the right place. I am sure that you can relate to a time when you had to concentrate on something of real importance and you had to look within to find the answer.

The intuitive mind sets in and will arrive at a conclusion without reason or knowledge; however it will possess a knowing. When intuition visits, welcome it, for it shall visit more frequently when activated.

ZEST

When I say the word zest! It brings a smile to my face; it just makes me think of bright, zingy lemon peel that adds a burst of freshness and energy to things. Being Zesty is like that   it means living your life full of energy, bursting with vitality and freshness. Living with Zest makes you feel alive, and full of life, it makes you feel free, joyful and uninhibited; it's what separates the mundane moments in life from the truly spectacular. If you want to achieve mastery, you must learn how to live a zestful and energetic life. Living with zest also means taking chances and taking risks, as any successful person can tell you, 'the larger the risk, the larger the reward'.

Here are a few ways for us to live our life with more zest and enthusiasm.

1. Become an unlimited being.

2. Experience new things every week, a new food, a new song, walk down a new street.

3. Intensify your best, be outstanding all of the time.

4. Fall in love with yourself and your life; remember this is a love that will last you a life time.

ZEAL

To live with Zeal is to be eager and enthusiastic about achieving a particular goal. In order to achieve mastery we need to learn to focus on our goals with zeal and passion and energy. The concept of Zeal originated with religion, and it means to be enthusiastic and eager to serve our religion or our faith. People with a lot of faith; automatically communicate their passion and belief to other people because of the zeal with which they believe in their religion.

Independent business owners and people who are passionate about what they do also display the zeal to succeed at business. Athletes who desire to win exhibit zeal while competing. Many artists and singers have zeal when they are performing.

Zeal is like a fire that is lit under you that makes you want to achieve your goals. It is the source for incredible passion and internal motivation. If you love what you do and believe in what you do, chances are that you can bring zeal into your life.

Zeal is what makes you get out of bed at 5am in the morning to go for a run and it is what keeps me working till 2am some nights. Even on days when I have had little rest I find time to work on this program simply because I am passionate about it and I believe in this program. I am zealous about the fact that it can help people aspire to mastery and make a positive difference to their lives.

Having Zeal to me is also to celebrate every single success that I have in my life. Reward yourself for your successes no matter how small or great they are. The very fact that you have listened to this program on Aspiring to Mastery and you are starting to apply the techniques you are learning is a great reason to celebrate and reward yourself. Each time you master and improve upon these life principles reward yourself. How will you celebrate?

Exercises on how to apply the 3 Z's of Zen, Zest and Zeal to your life can be found in your A-Z of Mastery workbooks.

Now would be a great time to do the exercises in your work book section as you are also guided with the following chapter.

CHAPTER EIGHT

SUMMARY AND REVIEW

In chapters one and two we discussed what the concept of Mastery really is, I also shared with you some personal stories from my life as a Master Neuro Linguistic Programmer, Master Coach, Thought Field Therapist / Emotional Freedom Therapist, Trainer and Inspirational Speaker. I will again reiterate that the principles outlined in this program can be used in all areas of your life where you would like to achieve mastery – business, relationships, personal development, spiritual, physical health and wealth.

Remember that your subconscious mind is the most faithful servant you will ever have in your life. Whatever programs you decide to run on it, whatever beliefs you hold true in your mind, your subconscious mind will strive to manifest in reality.

You really do have unlimited potential and in this program I am confident we have been able to help you use some of this unlimited potential towards manifesting everything that you desire. It is useful for us to remember that the world without is a mirror reflection of the world within, and I am certain that this program has helped you to shine up your internal mirror and consequentially brightened up your outer world.

I am sure by now you have realized that the road to mastery is paved with challenges and in order for you to practice the principles and concepts in this program you would have had to challenge and change many of the habits and mental patterns that were dear to you. For this I commend you.

In chapter three we discussed concepts from the letter A – E. Action is the single most vital factor that sets apart the dreamers from the achievers of their dreams. We talked about Newton's three laws of motions and their applicability to mastery. The first being that we will continue to remain static unless we take action! The second law states that the bigger the action the bigger the result and the third law states that not only do we work towards to our goals; our goals also pull us towards them.

Famous individuals including Walt Disney, Mahatma Gandhi, Thomas Edison, are prime examples of people who took action in order to achieve their goals. Remember my definition of action – 'an action is any act committed by us; either mental or physical that brings us closer to our goals in some way'. We also discussed the two types of action – mental and physical and how they are both important for us to achieve mastery.

In your workbooks you practised writing a goal using the 6P's of writing a goal - Possible, Present, Personal, Positively stated, Performance related and Pen it down.

We also talked about breaking our goals into achievable milestones, and the importance of taking action every single day in order to achieve our goals.

Belief is the assumptions we make about ourselves, about our world, about the people we interact with and about how we expect things to be, our beliefs are what shape our thoughts, our conversations and our behaviours. The importance of belief is the difference between people who achieve great things and people who do not. Remember Lance

Armstrong and Henry Ford. We need to believe in ourselves, our goals and our dreams, the people around us and in the universe. In order to change our beliefs we need to change our thoughts. In your workbook, you completed a short quiz to help you recognize your current feelings about your beliefs. You then identified your beliefs, including the beliefs that are holding you back from achieving your dreams. We also explored the reason behind these beliefs, along with evidence to refute them. You then wrote down new empowering beliefs and developed affirmations to help you change your thoughts to match them.

Remember that the first step to achieving your dreams is having the courage to dream and to translate those dreams into action. We spoke about Nelson Mandel's extraordinary courage; confidence and commitment which helped him attain his goals. The exercise in courage in your workbook encouraged you to explore any times in your past when the lack of courage caused you to compromise on your dreams. You also explored times when you had great courage and the factors that lead to that. We also identified the five most empowering and highly impactive states you had at that time in your life and anchored these positive resources.

The second C is confidence; confidence comes from the belief that you are a unique and special individual with something wonderful to offer the world. It comes from knowing what you excel at and believing in your own strengths and abilities. Without confidence it will not be possible for you to achieve all that you desire in your life. In your workbook we talked about the reasons why you want to be more confident, why you think you are not as confident as you want to be, the things that would make you more confident, and you then learnt how to anchor and step into each of these qualities to make you more confident. You also learnt the top ten secrets to self-confidence.

The third C stands for commitment, without commitment to your goals and to mastery, it becomes very difficult to achieve either in your life. The very definition of Commitment says that "it is the act of binding yourself either emotionally, physically or intellectually to a course of action".

In your workbooks, the exercise on commitment helps you to evaluate your current level of commitment versus your desired level of commitment. You also wrote down the goals that you would be 100% committed to achieving sometime.

Remember that discipline is the stronger cousin of commitment. Discipline is doing things we don't like or have too in order to achieve our long-term goals. It is choosing long-term results over short-term pleasures. We talked about the theory of motivation and how discipline is the key for getting from the 'I should stage' to the 'I'm inspired, just try and stop me' stage. In your workbook you learnt the six-step process to help you build discipline into your life. This includes writing down your goals, identifying the motivation behind the goal, building habits around the goal, making to-do lists, don't be discouraged by setbacks, and re-framing your excuses into positive frames.

The last concept discussed in this chapter is education; by education we mean the concept of long-term and lifelong education. In education we discussed the life of Leonardo ad Vinci, one of the greatest masters of all time. We also talked about the various ways in which you can gain knowledge including pursuing courses from universities, reading books, listening to audio courses or books, and attending lectures and talks. In your workbook you identified the things that you would like to learn and master; you identified the benefits behind gaining this knowledge, and also drafted a plan for your learning for the next one year.

In chapter four, we started with forgiveness and the importance of forgiving first yourself, and then the people in your life. Learning to forgive is an important step of in releasing negative thoughts and emotions and filling your mind with positive thoughts instead. In your workbook you would have written down things that you have not been able to forgive yourself for to date, you would have also written down things you have not forgiven other people for as well. You then wrote and practised saying your forgiveness affirmations to help you release all the negative feelings.

From forgiveness we moved onto focus, and the first rule of focus which is "Wherever you are, be there". Remember that the more you focus on mastery and achievement the closer you will get to your goals. Like it was said in the move The Secret - whatever we focus on expands and grows. Remember that the best way to focus your thoughts is to write down what you are thinking. In your workbook you wrote down your goals, and then went through 8 ways to find more focus in your life. This includes writing down thoughts, goals and actions on paper, using positive affirmations, being present, focus on achievement, focusing on solutions, asking questions, knowing why, taking control of emotional and mental facilities.

Faith is the absence of doubt, faith in us, our abilities, our greatness and our potential. Without faith we will be unable to achieve our dreams. Positive affirmations are a key technique in building up our faith.

In your workbook, you learnt some tips on writing powerful and effective affirmations, these include relaxing and letting go of old patterns of thought, use 'I' statements, make sure it is positive and written in the present tense.

A goal is a specific, measurable achievement and that is the next concept that we spoke about in chapter four. Remember that goals should be written down and that they should be specific, measurable, obtainable, challenging and with a completion date. In your workbooks, you listed everything that you wanted to BE, then everything that you wanted to DO, and everything you wanted to HAVE. You will only get to really HAVE once you BE and DO first. This is really important to remember. You also learnt about how to break a 10 year plan down into a 5 year plan, a 3 year plan, a 1 year plan, a 6 month plan, a one month plan and a daily to-do list.

Gratitude is one of the most important keys to the law of attraction. Gratitude is the tool that helps us to manifest all that we desire in our lives. If we are grateful for the things we have in our lives right now and we have the ability to be grateful for the things that we will have in our lives, then these will manifest themselves. Some of the exercises on gratitude in your workbooks are – writing 10 things that you are grateful for first thing in the morning. Starting a gratitude journal and writing down

5 things that you are grateful for each day, alternatively you can use one page to list 5 things you are grateful for today and another page to list the 5 things you are grateful for that you are yet to receive.

After gratitude we talked about the concept of the holistic approach. In this approach we spoke about the idea that our body, mind and spirit are interconnected and that we need to spend our time and energy strengthening each of these facets of our lives in order to live a full and balanced life. In your workbook you discovered various ways to incorporate a more holistic approach in your life. You would have added 4 new things each week on from each category of wellness in your body, wellness in your mind, wellness in emotion, and wellness is spirit.

Another H in this chapter was Harmony, or the principle of balance in all areas of our lives, or the absence of upset in any area of our lives. The four aspects of our lives that need to be in harmony are what we say, what we think, what we feel and ultimately what we do. In your workbooks you were able to evaluate if any areas of your life are out of balance currently, and identified the reasons for this discord along with action items to bring this area back into harmony.

Inspiration as you will recall is the condition in which our mind and emotions are stimulated to a high degree of feeling or activity. Inspiration makes creation and completion of projects and activities really easy. In your workbook you discovered some great ways to be inspired, including what already triggers your inspiration.

There was also an exercise where we devoted each day of the week to stimulating a different sense, Monday – sight, Tuesday – sound, Wednesday – feelings, Thursday – aromas, Friday – tastes. On Saturday and Sunday we access and expand all five senses simultaneously. Another way to be inspired is to read about your role models and their lives, which books have you read so far?

To be Invincible is to cultivate a spirit which is undefeated or cannot be defeated. In order to be invincible we must first be intimately aware of our strengths and weakness and the things that make us – us. In your workbook you revisited all the successes and failures that you have had in your life. You also delved into the reasons why you may have failed in the past, and the reasons why you may have succeeded. The other secret to being invincible is the ability to be your own best friend and source of encouragement and motivation; hence you created your own 'ego' list full of things you love about yourself. I am confident that you are reading this list every day.

In order to achieve mastery, one key ability is the ability to be innovative and to create things. Being innovate is a trait that will be appreciated in all the areas of your life, especially in the professional and wealth spheres. In your workbook you learned questions to ask yourself when faced with a problem that you have been unable to solve: how can you make it better? How can you make it faster? How can you make it cheaper? How can you add value to it? Are there more effective ways of doing this? Can something else be used in its place? Can it serve an alternate purpose? Remember to carry around your innovation notebook to help you keep track of any inspiration or ideas you may have. Another way to brainstorm for solutions for the problem without stopping to evaluate them until later.

People who have achieved mastery in their lives are also imaginative and creative beings. Remember that whatever you can imagine in your life, will ultimately become your reality. So the more vividly you can imagine a situation, the faster it will manifest itself in your life. Some ways to be more imaginative include, recognizing and accepting that you have the potential to be an imaginative person. Use affirmations to make yourself believe that you are more imaginative. Identify the things you want to be more imaginative about, think about the subject until you can picture different situations and solutions. Create spontaneously with lego or a paint box. Play mind games. Daydream and brainstorm ideas to bring more wealth into your life.

Joy is a feeling of happiness and enthusiasm which makes it easier to attract the things we want into our lives. In your workbook you wrote down ways to attract more joy into your life, you also gave yourself permission to be more joyful and committed to bringing more joy into your life. In your workbook you wrote down five things which give you joy along with permission to bring joy into your life. I am confident you have done some of these actions by now.

In chapter five we talk about the letters K – P beginning with Kindness. It is important for us to be kind to both others and most importantly to ourselves. In your workbooks you identified some ways to be kind to yourself and corresponding ways to be kind to others. You also identified two random acts of kindness to complete in the week along with some random acts of kindness to complete during the week.

K also stands for Karma or the law of cause and effect, in this program we established that whatever we do right now in this life will shape the outcome of our life at some point in the future. In your workbooks you wrote about a time in your life when something may not have turned out as well as you thought it might have and the reason for this outcome. You also thought about what positive cause could have resulted in a positive outcome instead. You then identified all the good outcomes or effects that you wanted in your life and identified the causes that you need to commit to in order to manifest these results.

Leverage means using a tool to gain power or advantage in your life, in this program A-Z of mastery; we talk about leveraging our strengths, the people around us and the tools we can use. In your workbook, you did a short exercise to help you identify your strengths, and also how to leverage these strengths to achieve your goals. You then identified people who may be able to help you achieve your goals, along with tools that you can leverage to help you be more productive or automate your business.

Love is a vital aspect in our program A-Z of mastery, and by love we do not only mean the love you have for your family and other special people in your life. You must also love and accept yourself for the wonderful, glorious person that you are instead of finding fault or criticising yourself. Remember the affirmation from Brian Tracy's seminar – 'I love myself', I know you are saying this to yourself constantly. We also did an exercise where we replaced any anger, fear and resentment that we had with a huge golden cup of glowing love. Remember this – love should be your top priority. Visit, call or spend time with all those special people in your life that you love. Lastly we also identified more ways to bring more love into your life and the positive benefits of having more love in your life.

Our last and final L in this chapter was on Legacy or on the concept of leaving a positive, valuable contribution to those who have come into contact with you. In your workbook, you explored the lives of three famous people whom have left a lasting legacy according to you. After some thought you identified what it is that they left as part of this legacy. Using an exercise where you wrote your own obituary, you identified the things you would like to be remembered for in your life and in a unique twist , you made a commitment to start LIVING your own OBITURARY every single day of your life. I trust that you are enjoying living your life with the goal of leaving a legacy behind you.

In this chapter, we also spoke about the concept of a positive mindset and the value of having a positive mindset when setting out to achieve mastery in your life. In your workbooks, you identified a list of books, seminars and talks to help you develop a more positive mindset – how many have you attended or read already? You also developed and wrote down your own affirmations to help you maintain a healthy and positive mindset.

The term modelling refers to modelling somebody who already has the skill we desire and is successful at that skill. It is our conscious choice to copy or model the behaviour of others in order to achieve more in our lives. Remember the basis for this theory that "'modelling successful performance leads to excellence". In your workbook you listed down the names of successful people whose behaviour or skills you would like to emulate. You also determined the behaviours/qualities/habits which contributed to their greatness. Using this information you identified ways to incorporate this behaviour into your life to make you successful and help you achieve mastery. How has modelling worked for you so far? Are you having more positive results with this technique than you did before?

Being magnetic is all about exuding natural charisma, self-confidence and incredible positive energy. Being magnetic makes it easier to achieve your goals, easier to persuade and interact with other people, and hence easier to achieve mastery in your life. In your workbook you completed an exercise on how to be more like a magnet drawing people towards you and being committed to being more magnetic in your life. There were also many suggestions for you on how to be more magnetic in your life and I am certain that these suggestions have worked for you.

A common activity that all masters perform at least once a day is meditation; meditation is the key to gaining clarity, calm and peace and is also the key to help you tap your intuition and attaining a sense of Zen, both concepts that we will review again shortly. In your workbook, I outline a simple technique to help you get started with meditation. I know that you have stuck to your commitment to meditate on a daily basis and that you are meditating on specific areas of your life and your goals each and every week. Do take some time to record your thoughts on meditation in your journal or at the back of your workbook.

Cultivating a never give up attitude is the key to overcoming feelings of self-doubt, and low self-confidence. It helps you view all the obstacles in your path and there will be many, as stepping stones to your success and an opportunity to learn and develop yourself. If you have stuck the words NEVER GIVE UP somewhere that you can see them then I know that they will provide you with that extra motivation every time the going gets tough. Recall now, your recordings from your workbook on the benefits of having a never give up attitude and the ways that you are keeping this attitude alive every day.

Time and time again in this program, we have talked about the fact that we become what we think we are. Therefore if you believe you are an optimist you most certainly are one and if you believe that you a pessimist than you are one. Remember that optimistic people are more positive most of the time, and in order to attract the things that you want in your life, you need to radiate positive vibrations. Hence it stands to reason that optimistic people have a better chance of attaining mastery and their goals than pessimistic ones. In your workbooks, we talked about the ways to become more optimistic and things that you can do on a regular basis to help you become and stay more positive.

Successful people are not afraid to be different, they know that it is their uniqueness and originality that helps them achieve success in their lives. In your workbook you identified 20 things that make you unique and special and from those 20 you identified six words that make you really stand out and make you – you. From these you crafted your identify statement. You also committed to performing one action every single day to express your uniqueness and identity for seven days. How did this make you feel?

Another key concept in the A-Z of Mastery is our belief in our own omnipotence, or our belief in our own ability to do anything we set out to do. We also spoke about how omnipotence is a self-fulfilling prophecy; if you believe you are omnipotent you are, and you will act in a way that actually reinforces this belief. I am confident that you are convinced of your own omnipotence. This principle is not only about belief, it is also about action, as time and time again you will need to step out of your comfort zone and face obstacles and your fears. In your workbook, you learnt a technique where you learnt to visualize your goals and determine if you are in your comfort zone, stretch zone or panic zone. You also learned how to identify obstacles you anticipate encountering and ways to deal with them. You also learnt how to stretch yourself to achieve more even if you were in your comfort zone.

The first letter in chapter six is P and stands first and foremost for Purpose, every master is aware of the purpose in his or her life. Without purpose there would be no passion, no motivation and no burning desire to take action and achieve their goals. In your workbook, you completed a fabulous exercise to help you find your purpose in life, this included identifying your talents and abilities and isolating the ones that give you joy, passion, motivation, inspiration, pleasure, happiness, contentment and fulfilment. Through this exercise you will have been able to identify your ideal life purpose, and the actions you can take towards living this life purpose.

Passion is a vital ingredient to achieving mastery in your life, without passion you will lack that necessary energy that comes from putting in more of you into everything that you do.

This energy is what separates a life of greatness from a life of mediocrity. You have already answered the question 'what are you passionate about', and found ways to do the things that you are passionate about each and every single day. You have also explored the possibility of doing the things that you are passionate about full time or for an extended period of time.

Since the beginning of this program, A-Z of mastery, I have spoken about each person's potential for greatness and mastery. In your workbook you were able to identify the insecurities and doubts do you have, which are preventing you from achieving your potential. You also formulated positive affirmations to help you overcome these fears and insecurities and I am certain that you are saying these to yourself every single day.

The final P is that of philanthropy. We have already talked about how many individuals who have achieved greatness are also great philanthropists. They put into practice the law of the universe, which is the more that you give of yourself and your resources to others, the more resources and riches will return to you. In your workbook, there was a selection of ideas to help you practice this principle in your life. I am certain that you have enjoyed practising these principles and that you have experienced the rich returns that being a philanthropist brings to your life.

In chapter six, we talked about two very interesting concepts, qualitative and being Quick Witted. In mastery it is all about the quality of things, versus the quantity. The more you focus on achieving your goal with a quality mindset, the more results you will achieve from them. Some places where it pays to focus on quality versus quantity are when working on critical projects for work, spending time with family, shopping for yourself and for groceries. Monitoring the TV you watch and the books you read to make sure they will indeed enrich your life. Making sure you have quality friendships and relationships that make you a better person, and that nurture and support you, versus many friends, who are never there for you in times of need.

Being quick witted is about being more knowledgeable, and being able to think on your feet. It is a quality that is much admired in business, and like all things in this program you can teach yourself to be more quick witted by reading more, observing more, learning more, and being more intuitive and impulsive.

I am certain that you have realized that you are 100% responsible for your life, and the people and circumstances that are in your life right now. I want you to always remember that you are responsible for who you are, your thoughts, your attitude, your feelings, your health and well-being and the people and relationships that you choose to have. In your workbook, you completed a fantastic exercise which would have given you some insight into how taking responsibility for your actions can have an impact on your life.

R also stands for Rigour, by rigour we mean to use tenacity, and you re-member we talked about that as well, to continue doing something till it gets done. It also means to maintain the same amount of effort on a project from the beginning to the end. Remember that the first step to maintaining rigour is to have a plan in place, along with milestones and rewards built in. You must also be determined to commit to and stick with your plan no matter what. This means that even on the days you really don't feel like doing something, you still do it anyway.

We have already established in an earlier part of the program, that in-ternal motivation is many times stronger than external motivation ever could be. One of the strongest ways to motivate yourself is to identify your reasons behind doing things. Once you know and understand your reasons behind your actions, you are more motivated to continue with the action.

I am sure you have heard it said, that every problem has a solution, you just need to find the right one. Very often the reason we don't find so-lutions to our problems, is because we focus on the problem and what caused the problem, versus what are possible solutions. Remember to always focus on what you can do to solve your problem and not look outside for solutions.

A good personal strategy is like a good strategy for a corporation, it is a clear cut plan with defined objectives that you want to achieve and goals that you wish to accomplish. Remember the ways to evaluate your strategy in your workbook using TOTE, or Test, Operate, Test and Exit. Did you use TOTE with the three goals that you had listed in your workbook? What did you do to achieve your outcome? What was the result of using this strategy versus your old ways of doing things?

Systems are a way to ensure that work is being carried out according to an established process. I love this acronym for SYSTEM – Saving you stress, time and money. Systems include automation, service standards, performance evaluation and time keeping. After completing the exercise on systems in your workbook, you would have had a chance to implement them in your life. Ask yourself what impact systems have had on your productivity, and in helping you achieve your goals.

I know that by now you have become a person of spirit, a person whose life is committed to and filled with vitality, energy, enthusiasm, and confidence. I know that this has had a positive impact on your happiness, health, wealth and power and had a positive impact on your personal and professional relationships. I am happy that you took the step in your workbook, to being committed to living with a spirit of higher consciousness, and I am positive that you are living this commitment each and every single day.

I have said before, and I will say again, the road to mastery is paved with obstacles, the very fact that you purchased this program, have completed the exercises in the workbook and are now on the last leg of the program, proves to me and to you, that you are a person of immense courage and strength, with an equally strong desire to change and enrich your life. You have and will however face setback and be constantly challenged, at times you will be filled with doubt, fear, and distress. It is in these times that I want you to remember to draw on your inner strength, which will help you to remain, positive, focussed and strong despite the odds. Remember that whenever you are paralysed with fear, you can ask yourself, what is the absolute worst thing that will happen? Now find a solution to that worst thing. How can I prevent it? Chances are that worst thing will never happen; however your inner strength and confidence will grow each time you cross a hurdle and achieve your goals.

Like gratitude and philanthropy, another little known secret to attracting wealth and success into your life is the secret of service. If you are of service to others, you will find that the universe will do it's best to be of service to you, and why wouldn't you want the universe at your service. Remember the questions you answered in your workbook about how can you help people, how can you be of service to them, how can you help others make money, how can you be of service to your employer, your internal and external customers and everybody else that you encounter every day. I am confident that you have put the principle of service to good use in your life and that it is helping you attract unlimited wealth and success.

The last letter on chapter six is T, and the first principle we spoke about was Tenacity, remember that tenacity is the courage and persistence to do something over and over again until you reach your goals. Tenacity is the key to developing habits. In order to be tenacious you must first identify your goal and the reason behind it. Identify the routines and habits that will help you to achieve this goal, understand why it pays to be more tenacious and really commit to being tenacious in your life. In your workbooks, you completed an in-depth exercise on being more tenacious.

In the movie The Secret you have heard it said that "thoughts become things", thoughts are all powerful, physical things that go out into the universe and come back as our reality. Remember the concept of BE, DO, HAVE, or how you need to BE before you can DO and Do before you can HAVE. In your workbooks, you identified the thoughts you need to have in order to manifest your dreams? You also need to DO your positive affirmations in order to manifest them. Lastly you must be ready and mentally prepared to have what you ask for, which means if you ask for a red Ferrari however constantly imagine your fuel bills, or parking challenges, you're not ready to HAVE that car and the universe will not attempt and manifest it into reality for you.

We respect many of the great masters and leaders, because of their integrity or their ability to tell the truth across most situations. In the same way being truthful is an important factor in achieving mastery. Remember that though it is sometimes difficult to tell the truth there are three situations in which you absolutely must tell the truth: We must tell the truth when people have the right to know the truth such as when selling someone a new service or product. Second, we must tell the truth with the relationships we are in be it our spouse, business partner, clients customers etc. Thirdly – we must tell the truth to people if their well-being depends on that truth. Remember the question you answered in your workbook, how you think your life has changed now that you have committed to telling the truth as often as possible both to yourself and to others.

In chapter seven, we begin with a discussion on the concept of a universal mind or shared consciousness, that we all have the ability to tap into. This energy can help us find answers to our questions and also manifest our dreams. One of the best ways to tap into this is meditation, by now you must have been meditating for a few days. How has this changed your life, do you find yourself able or ready to tap into this consciousness? Have you used any of the other techniques to tap into the universal mind? Above all remember to have faith that it exists and can and will work for you.

Do you now believe that you are unstoppable, one of my goals of creating this program, is to impart in you a sense of wonder at your own unlimited potential and also the belief that you can achieve ANYTHING you want to and that you are unstoppable. If you believe this then I am convinced that I have achieved my goals. Remember that to be unstoppable you must have passion, and like you identified in your workbook, you must believe that your goals are important. Lastly like so much in this program, you must have the commitment to follow through on your goals no matter what.

Many a times, if you look back at your failure to achieve a goal, you will find that the goal was not in alignment with your values, and hence your subconscious conspired to prevent you from achieving it. In your workbook, you identified your top ten values and wrote them down. You also ranked them in order of importance in your life, and evaluated which of your goals matched your values and changed the ones that didn't. Were you able to achieve these goals after aligning them with your values?

A powerful vision can be a powerful force that can shape you life and direct it where you want to go. A personal vision statement is your own personal compass, which can guide your decisions each and every day and also give you a long-term goal to work towards. Remember that your vision contains all the elements that make you – you, your passions, beliefs, goals and values.

You have already written your vision statement using the exercise in your workbook; I am sure that you are referring to it every day, especially when making important decisions. I trust that you had fun creating your vision board and that it is now displayed somewhere that you can see it every day, in fact as much of your day as possible. Remember that you can always add to your vision board. Remember to include your vision board in your daily meditation sessions.

The movie The Secret, was filled with advice about vibrations and the important of racing your vibrations to match that of the things you want to attract. Positive vibrations such as love, peace, balance, harmony, joy within you will raise your vibration. Everything is energy that vibrates at a different frequency. In your workbook you learnt about the different vibrational steps, including how to acknowledge the step you are currently on and how to move from one step to the next until you reach the final step of freedom, joy, happiness, and empowerment. I am certain that if you have tested these out then you are constantly using the ways I included in the workbook on how I quickly raise my vibration when I feel it is not matching the state I want to be in.

We already spoke that to be full of spirit, you need to be full of vitality, and this increases your energy levels, along with your self-esteem and ability to achieve mastery. In your workbook, I have listed 12 ways for you to become full of more vitality, I am confident that you have incorporated most of them into your daily life. Have you started eating in a way that makes you feel full of vitality. Remember the level of vitality you committed to being, how much closer to this level are you today?

Will if you remember is your inner strength for self mastery and decisiveness. It is your ability to overcome excuses, laziness, and procrastination. In your workbook, you have already identified the times when you have lacked willpower. You have also listed ways to increase your willpower, I am sure you have continued to put these actions into practice every day.

Remember that to be considered full of wisdom is to have the true meaning and understanding of things to enable you to humbly reason and make wise choices and decisions. You have already identified ways to cultivate your wisdom.

Wealth is not about money; rather it is not only about money, it is more about the feeling of abundance you get when you evaluate every area of your life. In your workbooks, you identified your abundance on a scale of 1-10, in the various areas of your life, personal, professional, spiritual, environmental, and financial. If you are using your money affirmations for accumulating wealth, then you are on your way to attracting wealth and prosperity. I am sure that you have realized that your wealth is YOUR responsibility and have written and started working towards the figure that means financial freedom for you. Have you implemented any of the ideas you had for wealth creation yet?

In your workbook you identified what the x-factor means for different people and what your own unique x-factor is. How have you been celebrating your x-factor every day?

In this program, yen is the strong desire to achieve your dreams. The key to having a powerful yen is to visualize your goals in great detail until you can identify what is your powerful driving force. You also identified ways to make your desire work for you constantly and keep you motivated. How strong is your yen today?

Zen is another Japanese concept that essentially means operating from a state of meditation or from the 'zone' as many of us call it. Remember that Zen is reached by meditating and by modelling our environment to reflect our mind.

Are you fresh and bright and full of sunshine like a lemon? Are you full of zest? Remember that living with zest raises your vibration and helps you attract more of what you want into your life. There is a great exercise associated with zest in your workbook that helps you identify all the positive vibrations in your body. You worked on your 'breakthrough', the one which defines ultimate success. You also identified how you would achieve this change in your life and how you would feel once you have achieved it.

The last concept in our program is that of zeal, remember that being full of zeal is like having a fire lit under you, which makes you want to achieve your goals. I would like to say what I said in your workbook. You are an amazing unlimited being.

It is time to CELEBRATE as though you have achieved ALL OF YOUR DREAMS ASPIRATIONS AND GOALS. Step inside your dream now. Live your dream now. What are you doing, what are you saying to yourself, what are other people saying to you, what house are you living in, what car do you drive, who is with you in your dream, what do you see, what purpose are you living with, what aromas are around you, what food do you taste, how much more have you learnt, how much love, joy, confidence passion and harmony do you have, how are you serving others, what ideas did you come up with, what are your thoughts, what colours are in your dream, what is your X Factor, how high is your vibration just how WEALTHY are you!

Celebrate all that you have achieved and say as many times as you like

THANK YOU, THANK YOU, THANK YOU

FOR ALL THAT I ASKED FOR,

FOR ALL THAT I BELIEVED IN,

FOR ALL THAT I RECEIVED.

You can now complete your mastery journal with your learnings and thoughts about this program along with your action steps, challenges and successes that you have experienced as a result of this program.

This brings us to the end of chapter eight, Congratulations, I am very proud of the work you have done with me on this program – Aspiring To Mastery. You have finished the final chapter of the A – Z of Mastery, I am confident you have enjoyed reading it and that together we have discovered some new thoughts and ideas for you to implement in your life. In chapters 3 – 7, we have explored the different elements that make up mastery and together we have worked on exercises to incorporate mastery into your life. I am sure that you have found it quite fascinating how these principles of mastery all interrelated. They are joined together. They belong together. Continue to work with these very special and fundamental life principles every single day. They will serve you well. Thank you for undertaking this journey with me and I celebrate your commitment and success and I am sure that these principles will help you to achieve your life of mastery just as they have helped me and my clients. Here is to your unlimited joy and success.

ASPIRING TO MASTERY
The Foundation

The Secret Laws Of Attracting Mastery into your life.

JACQUELINE DAY

WORKBOOK

WHY DO I WANT TO COMPLETE THIS PROGRAM?

Before you begin completing the corresponding exercises in your workbook, reflect upon and answer these questions.

Why do I want to complete this program – Aspiring to Mastery?

_____

_____

_____

_____

What are my expectations from this program?

_____

_____

_____

_____

What do I hope to achieve by the end of this program?

_____

_____

_____

_____

How do I see this program helping me in my life?

_____

_____

_____

_____

Are there any specific goals or outcomes I want to achieve upon completion of this program?

_____

_____

_____

_____

What is my level of commitment to this program, what am I willing to do to achieve mastery in my life.

_____

_____

_____

_____

What other questions or thoughts do I have about the program?

_____

_____

_____

_____

MY PERSONAL DECLARATIONS
FOR ASPIRING TO MASTERY

Example: I have a burning desire to aspire to mastery.

_____

_____

_____

_____

_____

_____

_____

_____

_____

_____

_____

_____

_____

_____

_____

_____

ACTION

It is paramount in order to achieve mastery in any aspect of your life whether it's personal or professional you need to set certain goals to achieve. It is only after you have achieved these goals that you feel you have achieved mastery in your life. As many famous a person would tell you, the first step to achieving any goals that we set for ourselves in life is to take action towards those goals.

In the space below write down one of your goals in specific terms, include dates, and time lines, and make it as specific as possible. Remember to use the 6 P's to goal setting: Possible, Present, Personal, Positively stated, Performance related and Pen it down.

Example: I am 10lb's lighter and am my ideal body weight on the **DAY MONTH YEAR**

My Goal:

_____

_____

_____

_____

Now break up this goal into achievable milestones, you can include dates or other guideposts.

If we take the example above then our milestones would be:

- ➢ Workout aerobically for an hour 3 times a week
- ➢ Do resistance training for an hour 3 times a week
- ➢ Give up sugar and desserts
- ➢ No junk food for three months
- ➢ Track food consumed daily
- ➢ Drink 8 glasses of water a day

	Milestones	Time-lines/Check posts
1		
2		
3		
4		
5		
6		
7		

Write down the action you are going to take TODAY to bring you one step closer to this goal and go out and take that action.

For example: Today I will work out for one hour in the gym.

_____

_____

_____

Write down the actions that you will take every single day for the next SEVEN days to bring you one step closer to your goal.

Our Example:

Day 1: Workout for an hour in the gym.

Day 2: Walk for half an hour.

Day 3: Workout for an hour in the gym.

Day 4: Workout for an hour in the gym.

Day 5: Go on a fruit diet today

Day 6: Walk for half an hour.

Day 7: Workout for an hour in the gym.

The key message here is ACTION is equal to ACHIEVEMENT so take ACTION today!

BELIEF

Remember what Michael Korda one of the most influential publishers and authors of his time said "To succeed, we must first believe we can".

The first step to incorporating the habit of belief in your life is to discover your beliefs and to discover if they serve you well.

1. Are your beliefs about yourself:

    Positive   Negative

2. Do they inspire you to become a better person?

    Yes   No

3. Do they make you feel miserable about yourself?

    Yes   No

4. Do you believe you are a unique, talented individual with something special to offer the world?

    Yes   No

5. Do you believe that you deserve to be happy?

    Yes   No

6. To be loved?

    Yes   No

7. To be wealthy?

    Yes   No

8. To be healthy?

    Yes   No

9. Do you believe that you have the right to do the work you love every day?

    Yes   No

10. Do you believe in your capabilities as a person?

    Yes   No

11. Do you believe you are smart, confident, an achiever, or an innovator?

    Yes   No

What are your beliefs? List them down here?

Example: One of your beliefs could be "Money is hard to make; money does not grow on trees."

_____

_____

_____

_____

_____

_____

_____

_____

_____

_____

_____

Which of your beliefs are preventing you from achieving mastery in your life, which ones would you like to change? Which of these beliefs are negative in nature –place a circle around them.

Example: The rich get richer and the poor get poorer. My belief about money is definitely holding me back from accumulating wealth in my life.

_____

_____

_____

_____

_____

_____

_____

_____

_____

_____

_____

_____

_____

_____

_____

_____

_____

Can you think of any reasons that have led you to develop these beliefs? Is this belief your own or have you inherited it from your parents, teachers, peers etc?

Example: All my life I have seen people struggle to make money, my parents always taught me that making money was hard and only the rich or the lucky ever made money easily.

_____

_____

_____

_____

_____

Can you think of any evidence to prove these negative beliefs wrong?

Examples: Everyday hundreds of people around the world are making more money than me from their ideas and through their hard work, many of these people come from worse circumstances than me, many of them are less talented than me, yet they all find it very easy to make and accumulate money.

_____

_____

_____

_____

_____

_____

What are the new empowering beliefs that you want to have in your life beginning today? Think, are there people in the world just like you who have achieved the things you want to achieve, can you use their example to fuel your belief?

Example: It is easy to make money; millions of people make money every day; money does grow on trees; money comes easily to me; I manifest money from many sources; I am abundant and deserve to be wealthy, it is my right.

_____

_____

_____

_____

_____

_____

_____

_____

_____

_____

_____

_____

_____

_____

_____

In order to make this new belief your reality, write down your belief twenty times every day, say it to yourself whenever you can, and place it predominantly where you can see it. The sooner you change your thoughts, the sooner your thoughts will become your beliefs, which will become your reality.

COURAGE

Answer these questions as truthfully as you can:

Before you can even begin to achieve your goals or dreams, you must first have the courage to dream and to put those dreams into action.

Write down a dream, a goal or a desire that you wish to achieve in your life and have not so far had the courage to follow it through?

_____

_____

_____

_____

_____

_____

_____

_____

_____

_____

_____

_____

What are some of the reasons that have prevented you from achieving this goal or dream?

For example – Are you afraid of taking the plunge, of believing in your dreams and your abilities; are you afraid of what people will say or what will happen?

_____

_____

_____

_____

_____

_____

Now think of some times in your life when you had great courage and followed through on your dreams, goals, and desires. Write them down now and vividly see, hear and feel what you experienced at the time you had so much courage.

_____

_____

_____

_____

_____

_____

What were the five most empowering and highly impactive states you had at that time in your life when you had so much courage? Write them down now. If you cannot recall them, think of the empowering states you would need to be courageous. Examples could be: powerful, in control, certain, confident, unstoppable. Take deep breathes in and out with each one of these five resources and place your hand on your chest or where ever feels comfortable to you and anchors these positive resources.

_____

_____

_____

_____

_____

Now go back to question one – the goal, wish or desire that you did not have the courage to pursue.

Take the five positive resources and transfer them into this particular goal. Breathe in and anchor these resources one at a time so that you are connected to them every time you think of this goal. Write down the first action you will take towards this goal now.

_____

_____

_____

_____

_____

Remember how you learned to ride your bike, courage is something that comes from within, and you must learn to tap into your own internal reserves of courage if you want to achieve mastery.

Resolve to accept the fear associated with the goal, and recognize that it is normal to be fearful, let it go and follow the steps of courage. Do something NOW to take you one step closer to this goal. Do something every day to bring you closer to achieving this goal. Take baby steps, use the Action technique to help you achieve the things you have always wanted to but have been holding back

CONFIDENCE

Confidence will help you become more effective as you are more certain about yourself. From this your relationships at work, home, and socially will attract good. You will accomplish more as people are naturally drawn towards you. Your vibration and energy will radiate conviction, faith, certainty, belief, self-reliance, fearlessness, trust. Before doing the exercise on how to build up your confidence, write down why you want to be more confident in your life:

Example: I want to be confident at public speaking.

_____

_____

_____

_____

_____

_____

_____

Why do you think you are not as confident as you would like to be, be honest when writing down your answers.

Example: I am not comfortable and that makes me shy in public.

_____

_____

_____

_____

_____

_____

_____

What would it take for you to become more confident? List down 5 or 6 resources that would make you more confident?

Example: calmer, connected, inspiring, awesome, joyful, professional. Imagine looking at yourself with all these qualities. Really connect with your feelings.

_____

_____

_____

_____

_____

_____

Take the first positive quality and step into it. Notice how you look, how you feel and what you are hearing. You want to increase this confidence, and as you experience this quality, step with it into the next quality. Do this until you have used all 5-6 resources. Each time increase the intensity of the confidence until you overflow with confidence. Breathe in and smile and anchor this feeling. Write down what this experience meant to you.

Write down again what you want to feel confident in and state these qualities positively. Then write down an action you will take.

Example: I now am totally confident when I speak in public. I am awesome and inspiring when I speak as I connect joyfully with my audience in a calm and professional manner. To continually develop my skills, I am joining a Toastmasters class on the **DAY MONTH YEAR.**

Here are our secret 10 steps to achieving more confidence in your life beginning today:

1. Dress to impress – dress like someone in power, wear clothes that make you feel confident and good about yourself.

2. Walk faster – confident people walk faster

3. Stand tall – maintain good posture

4. Advertise yourself – to yourself : make a list of all your positive attributes and read it out to yourself twice a day, use positive affirmations to help you become more confident, such as "I am a strong confident person in all that I do"

5. Instead of thinking about the things you don't have, think about the things you DO have, be grateful.

6. Look for the best in other people – give compliments; over time you will learn how to see the best in yourself as well.

7. Sit in the front next time you are in church, class or at a lecture, sit up front – overcome your fear of being in the limelight.

8. Speak Up – take an active part in discussions, don't be timid, and be brave.

9. Do some physical exercise so you are feeling good, energised and confident.

10. Be your own cheerleader – write down a mantra to repeat to yourself every time you find your confidence levels sagging. Say it every day as many times as you like until you begin to believe in it. Example: "I am confident, awesome and empowered".

COMMITMENT

The very definition of Commitment says that "it is the act of binding yourself either emotionally, physically or intellectually to a course of action".

Thomas Edison said "The successful person makes a habit of doing what the failing person doesn't like to do."

What is your current level of commitment to achieving your goals?

1. Low

2. Medium

3. High

What would you like your commitment level to be?

1. Low

2. Medium

3. High

Action will be delayed without commitment as it transforms your ideas, thoughts and dreams into action. How could you increase your commitment levels? What would you need to do to become more committed to your goals?

_____

_____

_____

_____

_____

What goals do you wish you were more committed to? Write them down here. Resolve to be 100% committed to these goals from today onwards. Follow the action exercise detailed earlier to help you achieve these goals.

I, _____ am 100% committed to achieving the following goals

_____

_____

_____

_____

_____

Signature & Date

DISCIPLINE

Why do we need discipline in our lives? Discipline is the stronger cousin of commitment. Discipline is doing things we don't like or have to in order to achieve our long-term goals. It is choosing long-term results over short-term pleasures.

Here is a six step process to build discipline into your life:

Step 1: Write down one of your goals in clear and simple language. Have a clear idea of what you want to achieve and by when.

_____

_____

_____

_____

_____

Step 2: Identify your motivation behind the goal, remember the motivation theory – identify whether the motivation is internal or external? In order to go from external motivators to internal motivators it will take a lot of discipline.

_____

_____

_____

_____

_____

Step 3: Build habits around your goal, by doing the same thing at the same time every day. Write down the time and the action here.

_____

_____

_____

_____

_____

Step 4: Make to – do lists for yourself that will bring you closer to goal achievement and stick to them. Write down everything you have to do in order to achieve this goal.

_____

_____

_____

_____

_____

Step 5: Do not be discouraged by slips and minor setbacks, recognize that it is all part of the process. Write down any excuses you may have for NOT being disciplined here. Recognize your excuses? What are the things that will keep you from doing what you have decided to do? What will affect your discipline? Write them down here so that you can recognize them easily.

_____

_____

_____

_____

_____

Step 6: When you have a minor setback, look at your excuses. How can you discipline and motivate yourself to continue? Positively frame your perspective. Ones I use are - "the end result will make this all worthwhile" "I can really see how this will turn out" "what else can I do to make this work". Write some of your positive frames here.

_____

_____

_____

_____

_____

EDUCATION

It is important for us to be lifelong learners. Without learning new things we stop expanding ourselves, we are unable to find new ideas or new ways of doing things and we become limited in our thoughts and outlook.

What are the things that you would like to learn and master? It could be a language, a new way of cooking, pottery, a sport, a new career, wealth creation?

_____

_____

_____

_____

_____

Write down the WIIFM or the "What's in it for you" for learning this new idea, topic, or subject. What do you feel are the benefits of this learning?

_____

_____

_____

_____

_____

Write down a plan to achieve your education goals for this year make it as comprehensive and detailed as you like. What do you NEED to do to learn this? Be committed to it 100%.

_____

_____

_____

_____

_____

Here are some ways to incorporate the habit of learning into your life:

Make a list of books you would like to read this year and buy two

Take a new course/cultivate a new hobby/learn a new sport

Attend a lecture or a talk by a leader you admire

Look for some classes on the internet that you can sign up for

Download or buy an audio course to listen to in your car

Write down any other ideas you may have

_____

_____

_____

_____

_____

FORGIVENESS

Only when you truly forgive will you make the transformations which will make the difference that makes the difference. Forgiveness starts with self forgiveness then forgiveness of anybody else in your life who has hurt you or caused you pain of any kind. This could be family members, teachers, close partners, business partners, work colleagues etc. Everybody has encountered pain or hurt at sometime in their life. To remain in a state of unforgivenesses increases that pain. The person you need to forgive may not be in your life any more. They are not bearing your pain. They are free. It is time that you set yourself free. Show a willingness to forgive as the Universe will acknowledge this willingness. Take another willingness step. Each step will lead you to full foregiveness and freedom. Set yourselffree now.

What are the things in your life that you would like to forgive yourself for but have not been able to until now?

_____

_____

_____

What are the things in your life that you are holding on to about other people and that you need to forgive?

_____

_____

_____

Now write your forgiveness affirmations:

Example: I totally forgive _____ for _____, and I now release and let go of all anger, pain and resentment. I am no longer a victim. I am totally free.

_____

_____

_____

Notice what your feelings are and be still with your feelings. Notice what you have learnt from the experience. Listen to the messages that you receive. Ask for forgiveness for holding onto the resentments.

Now look back at what you have written. Now write all of this exercise on a separate piece of paper. Place a cross through the exercise in the workbook. Take the separate piece of paper with your work transferred onto it. Burn the paper and say to yourself "As I burn this piece of paper I let go of any resentments and negative feelings that I have towards myself and towards others in my life, I forgive myself and I forgive others in my life, I am now free of this pain, resentment and negativity – I LET IT GO". Resolve to never think of these issues again, if they do crop up give them a different meaning so that they are a new program or focus on something instead. One great way to switch from hurt to forgiveness is to focus on the things you are grateful for instead.

FOCUS

Remember that what you focus on expands. What are the positive things in your life that you need to focus on more in order to manifest your goals? List them down here:

_____

_____

_____

_____

_____

_____

_____

Here are some ways to help you become more focussed in your life:-

1. Write your thoughts, goals and actions down on paper

2. Write and use your own positive affirmations

3. Resolve to be fully present in the moment regardless of what you are doing.

4. Focus on where you want to get to and what you want to achieve.

5. Focus on the solution

6. Ask yourself how you can turn something around and make a difference

7. Know your reason why

8. Take full control of your emotional and mental faculties

FAITH

Faith is a state of mind which grows in strength as you develop life principles and mastery. It is important that the sub conscious mind is fed with positive and constructive thought on a regular basis. Doing so will form a foundation for the expansion of all that you wish for in life. Faith is having that inner certainty and involves internalising new ways and patterns of thinking. One of the most powerful ways to build faith in our lives is through the use of positive affirmations. Write down your own positive affirmations for each area.

Here are some tips on how to write an affirmation:

1. Relax and let go of old patterns of thought.

2. Transform these old patterns into new positive programs of thought.

3. Focus on what you want not what you don't want.

4. Keep it as short as possible to keep you focussed.

5. Write in the first person, use 'I' statements

6. Write positive statements.

7. Make sure that it is in the present tense.

Some examples of affirmations:

I am confident in all that I do.

I am healthy and energetic.

I am wealthy and attract more wealth every day.

I live in harmony and peace every day.

Write down affirmations that help you have faith in your abilities:

_____

_____

_____

_____

Write down affirmations that help you have faith in your goals and ideas:

_____

_____

_____

_____

Write down affirmations that help you have faith in the things that you believe in:

_____

_____

_____

_____

GOALS

The difference between a dream and a goal is that dreams are often fleeting, or merely passing wishes that we do not work towards either consciously or unconsciously, while a goal is a specific, measurable achievement which you work towards sometimes both consciously and unconsciously.

The process of writing down your goals is what is most important. It has been established that there is a definite connection between your subconscious mind and the act of writing something down versus merely thinking it. Writing your goals down will help your sub-conscious mind manifest it faster than if you merely focussed on thinking about your goal in your head. Writing down your goal also helps you consciously work towards what you desire.

Goals should be:

1. Specific

2. Measurable

3. Obtainable

4. Challenging

5. Have a completion date attached

You can also write goals for the different areas of your life: career goals, financial goals, family goals, physical goals.

First take some time to write down every single goal you want to achieve over the next 10 years or more into the future. Write them as though you have already achieved them. As you write notice how you feel, what you see, what you can hear, what is going on around you.

List everything that you want to BE.

_____

_____

_____

_____

_____

_____

List everything that you want to DO.

_____

_____

_____

_____

_____

List everything that you want to HAVE.

_____

_____

_____

_____

_____

_____

The following guide will help -

Write your BE list as descriptive nouns; for example – I am an inspirational leader.

Write your DO list as a verb; for example – I empower people and change their life. These are the actions you take in order to HAVE.

You will only get to really HAVE once you BE and DO first. This is really important to remember. What will BEING and DOING let you HAVE in your life?

I will now show you how you can further break down a ten year plan into a to-do list that you follow every single day. It is important to take action every day towards your goal accomplishment. Write as many goals as possible for you to achieve over the next ten years. Usually I ask my clients to write at least 101 goals and I advise that you do the same. Some of these goals you want to achieve in one month, some you want to achieve in ten years.

For each goal you will need to write a positive affirmation using the rule of the six P's To remind you, they are Possible, Present, Personal, Positively stated, Performance related and Penned down.

Example: One goal may be to get a Ph.D. from a premier university in the next ten years.

MY 10 YEAR PLAN

Example: It is **DAY MONTH YEAR** and I am qualified with my Ph.D.

_____

_____

_____

_____

MY 5 YEAR PLAN

Example: it is **DAY MONTH YEAR** and I have my Masters degree.

_____

_____

_____

_____

MY 3 YEAR PLAN

It is **DAY MONTH YEAR** and I have purchased all the books I need for my studies.

_____

_____

_____

_____

MY 1 YEAR PLAN

Example: I have researched Graduate programs and have written the entrance exams.

_____

_____

_____

_____

MY 6 MONTH PLAN

Example: I have filled in the application forms and sent them to the university.

_____

_____

_____

_____

_____

MY ONE MONTH PLAN

Example: I study every day to write the exam.

_____

_____

_____

_____

_____

MY DAILY TO DO LIST

Example: I study from 8 – 12 noon every day for the entrance exams

_____

_____

_____

_____

_____

Use the Law of Attraction to write your goals. For this write your goals down as if you already have achieved them and write them in positive language. A positive intention is one of the secrets of manifestation.

An example of a well written goal using this technique is this: "I, Jacky have a wonderful relationship with all my clients and make a positive impact on each one of their lives". Notice that the goal is written using an 'I' statement, and also as if I have already achieved my goal. This language enables the universe to manifest my goal. Write your goals using language that is positive and in the present tense to help manifest your goals more quickly as the universe works to make it come true. Act as if you have achieved your goals. Have positive expectation.

Start taking action on the goals that you know you believe in. The achievement of these will move you forward to those bigger goals as your belief vibration expands.

What goals do you want to achieve using these techniques write them down here, keeping the guidelines in mind?

_____

_____

_____

_____

_____

GRATITUDE

Remember that gratitude is a fundamental key to the Law of Attraction.

Why is gratitude such a powerful tool? Gratitude is the expression of a positive emotion that we feel in relation to a goal. Gratitude allows you to accept and acknowledge the value of something in your life. When you accept the value of something- you stop resisting it and it becomes real in your life. Gratitude is a tool when used correctly can help you manifest the things that you want into your life.

Be grateful for what you have right now! Then you prepare yourself for the gratitude you will have for the things that are on their way to you.

Technique one: as soon as you wake up in the morning write down ten things you are grateful for that day.

- I am grateful for my health.

- _____

- _____

- _____

- _____

- _____

- _____

- _____

- _____

- _____

Technique Two: Buy and start a Gratitude journal. Every day write down five things that you are grateful for today. Make this a part of your to-do list so that you don't forget. The 5 things must be 5 different things every single day. Never duplicate anything.

Technique Three: In your gratitude journal use one page to list 5 things you are grateful for right now, and on the other page list things you are imagining that you are grateful for in your future. What a great way to manifest the things you want. This can be quite powerful too. I have included an example for you to learn from.

I am happy and grateful for: (list 5 things you already have)

- For the house that I live in

- The car that I drive

- A warm heated house

- The healthy food that I eat

- My family and friends

I am happy and grateful for: (list the things you want to have in the future)

1. My holiday to France

2. Weighing my ideal weight

3. A new corporate client contract

4. I am the author of a best selling book

5. My new home

_____

_____

_____

_____

_____

HOLISTIC APPROACH

In the holistic approach we acknowledge that all aspects of our body, mind and spirit are interconnected and that we need to spend our time and energy strengthening each of these facets of our lives in order to live a full and balanced life. Here are some ways that you can adopt a more holistic approach to the way you live your life. Check them off as you incorporate them into your life. Commit to doing one thing from every category this week. That's 4 new techniques that you will adopt to help you lead a more holistic life this week.

Write out an affirmation to help you adopt a more holistic approach here. An example of one I often use is – I balance my life between work, rest and play. They all get equal time.

_____

_____

_____

_____

_____

Focus on wellness in your body:

1. Exercise

2. Healthy eating

3. Natural medicines and treatments

4. Proper sleep

5. Time to relax and destress

6. Therapies such as natural wellness therapies and massage therapies

Focus on wellness in your mind:

1. Focus on thinking positive thoughts

2. On being more optimistic

3. On enriching your mind through reading or exploring new ideas

4. On being more creative and meditating or mentally relaxing your mind

Focus on wellness in emotion:

- By caring for and nurturing yourself

- By acknowledging and dealing with your emotions

- By expressing your emotions to people around you

- By journalising them or some other form of self expression

Focus on wellness in spirit:

1. By spending time alone in quiet reflection

2. Enjoying nature

3. Praying or any other type of religious ritual that works for you

4. Enjoying the moment no matter where you are and what you are doing.

HARMONY

Harmony essentially means being in balance in all the areas of our lives or in other words it is the ABSENCE of discontent or upset in our lives. Opposite to harmony is discord. Harmony must start within us.

Whenever you feel out of balance or not in harmony evaluate if all the four aspects of your life are in balance with each other. The four aspects are:

1. What we say – the words we use to talk about things

2. What we think – our thoughts about things and people

3. What we feel - our feelings

4. What we do – our actions

If you are feeling discontent, chances are that one of these aspects is out of sync with the others and you have to only alter that aspect to be in harmony once more.

Check that all aspects of your life are in balance or harmony with each other. Check the areas of your life that you feel are in harmony right now from the list below.

- Financial

- Career and relationships at work

- Love and intimacy

- Personal environment and organization

- Personal, professional and spiritual development

- Health and Well being

- Family and Friends

- Recreation and free time

If you have left any of the boxes unchecked, ask yourself what are the possible reasons that this area is out of balance.

_____

_____

_____

_____

_____

_____

What can you do to bring this area into harmony with the other aspects of your life, list your action steps here:

_____

_____

_____

_____

_____

_____

Take action now to bring more harmony into your life.

INSPIRATION

What is inspiration? The dictionary definition of Inspiration is a condition in which our mind or emotions are stimulated to a high degree of feeling or activity. When we are inspired we are able to create new things and start or complete projects and activities with ease.

Here are some ways to be inspired:

1. What triggers your inspiration? Aim to repeat this experience when you get stuck. For me reading quotes inspire me, every time I get stuck I read some inspirational quotes for a few minutes. Another great way to awaken my inspiration is to listen to the masters of classical music. Write down what triggers your inspiration here:

_____

_____

_____

_____

_____

_____

2. Access and expand a different sense on every day of the week. Make this your predominant sensory acuity for the day. Process information meaningfully. Notice what you notice. Monday – sight, Tuesday – sound, Wednesday – touch, Thursday – aromas, Friday – tastes. Saturday and Sunday access and expand upon all five senses. For each day of the week write down what inspirations you gained from expanding your awareness of each sensory activity. What insights did you

gain? What did you notice that you had not noticed before? What new ideas, thoughts and inspirations did you acquire

Monday: _____

_____

Tuesday: _____

_____

Wednesday: _____

_____

Thursday: _____

_____

Friday: _____

_____

Saturday: _____

_____

Sunday: _____

3. Read upon your role models. What was it that inspired them? What lessons of theirs can you apply in your life to increase your inspiration?

4. Which one of your role models will you commit to read about this week?

_____

_____

_____

INVINCIBLE

To be invincible is to have an 'invincible' spirit, or a spirit which cannot be defeated, a spirit that is unconquerable despite the hardships, adversities and trials we might face throughout our lives.

In order to be invincible, we must first seek self-knowledge, since only when we know ourselves intimately can we be strong enough to overcome all hardship. We must be intimately familiar with all our success and our perceived failures.

In the columns below, write down a list of all your success and perceived failures in your life. Fill in as much as you can.

My Successes	My Perceived Failures

The things you think you failed at, write down why you think this was.

_____

_____

_____

_____

_____

The successes that you had, write down what it was that made you succeed.

_____

_____

_____

_____

_____

The resources that made you successful, if you had used these in the areas you had a perception of failure or given up on, what difference would it have made to the results you would have had? How will you use these resources the next time you are about to quit!

_____

_____

_____

_____

_____

Secondly, you must love yourself; only if we love ourselves enough do we become invincible to the on-slaughter of others and also the constant bombardment from the media, which urges us to be thinner, taller, richer, or better looking. Love yourself and such things will not matter. Create your own 'self esteem' list, or things that you love about yourself. Refer to this every day to create your invincibility. Carry it around with you.

What I love about myself:

- _____

- _____

- _____

- _____

- _____

- _____

- _____

- _____

- _____

- _____

- _____

- _____

- _____

- _____

- _____

- _____

- _____

- _____

- _____

Don't you feel great that you have so much love for yourself? Write down your feelings here.

_____

_____

_____

_____

INNOVATION

In order to be innovative, allow yourself to be creative, and take steps to incorporate creativity into your daily life. Whether it is by painting a picture, writing in a journal or taking up a hobby like pottery or craft making. Be creative in your life purpose or career.

Think of a problem you have wanted to solve lately, and now ask yourself these questions:

How can this be made better?

_____

_____

_____

_____

How can it be made faster?

_____

_____

_____

_____

How can it be made cheaper?

_____

_____

_____

_____

How can I add value to this?

_____

_____

_____

_____

What more effective ways are there of doing this?

_____

_____

_____

_____

What else can be used in its place?

_____

_____

_____

_____

What other purpose can it serve?

_____

_____

_____

_____

One of the most essential tools for being innovative is keeping a notebook to note down ideas, thoughts, stories, quotes, pictures and other inspirations.

_____

_____

_____

_____

Another way is to constantly remind yourself to think outside the box, or to brain-storm for ideas, don't dismiss or evaluate them at the time. Just write down the problem or challenge and write down all the solutions that occur to you. Do this now:

My challenge is _____

_____

How can I be innovative?

_____

_____

_____

IMAGINATION

Creative people often find it easy to imagine things in the eye of the mind, and it is no secret that whatever the human mind can conceive it can then go on to make a reality. It is through imagination that the human race has evolved and created unlimited inventions. Great masters, leaders, musicians, artists, inventors all had an imagination so great and creative with a will so strong that their vision became a reality. Tuning into the subconscious mind and paying attention to those instincts and hunches made them receptive to the possibilities of their creations.

There are many ways to stretch your imagination and these are some of them:

1. Recognize and accept the fact that you have the potential to be imaginative. Picture yourself being imaginative; start listing that as an attribute you possess - truly believe in your ability to be imaginative. Write an affirmation for you to become more imaginative. One I use is – I tap into my unlimited mind of creation and draw from it the right thoughts plans and actions that will lead me to my ultimate success.

_____

_____

_____

_____

_____

2. Imagination is regular constant use of the mind. Just as when you exercise physically, when you exercise mentally, your imagination muscles will be stretched and toned and the more imaginative you will become.

    _____

    _____

    _____

    _____

    _____

3. What do you want to be more imaginative about? Is it a maths problem? A work of art? Planning a special occasion? Your ultimate goal?

    _____

    _____

    _____

    _____

    _____

4. Once you have chosen a subject, read about it, do research and encourage yourself to 'THINK' and contemplate what you are reading about.

5. Create spontaneously: buy Lego, clay, a paint box, create a collage and let your imagination run wild. Interpret your creation, give it a meaning. The key is to unleash your creative imagination.

6. Exercise your mind: take any common item like a paper clip or a safety pin. Write down 20 ways you can use this item, encourage yourself to think as creatively as possible.

_____

_____

_____

_____

_____

7. Day dream: spend some time each day imagining your life, your perfect job or anything that appeals to you. It's your imagination and it can be as unrealistic and stretching as you want it to be. There are no rules in your imagination. Never think 'impossible' when you are day dreaming, instead everything becomes 'possible'.

8. Use your imagination to create ideas for wealth creation in your life. What thoughts, ideas could bring wealth into your life? Everything starts with an idea. Brainstorm six ideas that you could develop right now. Use your imagination!

_____

_____

_____

_____

_____

JOY

Joy is that feeling of happiness and enthusiasm which you experience when you feel that all is well with your world. When we are joyful we feel enthusiastic, and abundant. When we are full of joy we are also more easily able to attract the things we want into our life.

What do you think are the advantages of bringing joy into your life? Write them down now.

_____

_____

_____

_____

_____

_____

_____

Give yourself permission to be joyful in your life. Choose 5 or 6 things from the list below or write your own, that will really bring joy into your life. Really commit to bringing more joy into your life from today onwards.

Here are some easy ways to bring more joy into your life, be sure to check them off as you do each one of them.

- Pamper yourself with a Spa treatment or a massage

- Go for a walk in nature

- Play with your pet

- Do something kind for someone

- Spend time with people you love

- Watch a funny movie or read a funny book

- What inspires you? Many times the things that inspire us also bring us joy.

- Be in the moment

- Make a to do list and celebrate as you complete each activity

- Do something for you – buy yourself a present or treat yourself to something you want.

- Join a dance class

Now write at least five things for which you give yourself permission to bring joy into your life. Date the action so you know you will commit to this. You can bring joy into your life right now, this very moment! An example of mine is – I Jacky give myself permission to go to a dance class at 7.30 this evening. I have fun and express my joy.

_____

_____

_____

_____

_____

_____

KINDNESS

If we are to achieve mastery in our lives, we must first learn how to be kind to others and most importantly to ourselves. As Amelia Earhart said, kindness is like a chain reaction, one kind action leads to another and eventually it all comes back to us tenfold."

We must first start by being kind to ourselves before we can be kind to others; here are some ways to be kind to yourself.

1. Remember that you cannot change the past; you cannot predict the future however you can live in the present. Resolve to let go of past fears and disappointments, stops worrying about the future and instead let yourself focus completely on the present.

Tell yourself that everything will work out well, it always does.

2. Do one thing at a time instead of multi-tasking

3. Schedule 20 minutes a day for yourself: write down your timeslot here _____

4. Let go of the problems and struggles that are just not worth it – focus your attention on ways to enhance your life.

5. Learn how to say NO to people who make unnecessary demands on your time and energy.

6. Find joy in your life

You can be kind to others by:

1. Not gossiping or partaking in rumours which can at times be unintentional.

2. LISTEN the next time someone talks, just listen without interrupting, pay attention and show a real interest in them.

3. Give out compliments – give someone a compliment today and see how it makes you feel. Moreover, how does it make the other person feel.

4. Perform random acts of kindness – do this today - buy a homeless person a cup of coffee, or buy some flowers for your co-worker. How does it feel to do this?

5. Volunteer or contribute to a charity on a regular basis

What two acts of kindness will you carry out this week that will make a difference to somebody else? Write them down here.

_____

_____

_____

What other acts of kindness will you commit to in the future?

_____

_____

_____

KARMA

According to the law of Karma, which is also known as the law of cause and effect, whatever we do right now in this life will shape the outcome of our life at some point in the future.

Think of the times in your life when something may not have turned out as well as you thought that it may have; a time when you have been disappointed, hurt or upset.

_____

_____

_____

What do you think you may have done either consciously or unconsciously that contributed to this outcome and effect?

_____

_____

_____

_____

What positive cause could you have created instead in order to attract a positive effect, and what was the lesson that you learnt?

_____

_____

_____

_____

Think of all the things you want in your life: all the good effects that you want.

List them down here: _____

_____

_____

_____

Now list all the things you need to do to obtain these 'effects' in your life, what will cause these effects to happen:

_____

_____

_____

_____

LEVERAGE

The dictionary definition of leverage means using something as a tool to gain power or an advantage. It is being able to exert a greater influence on a situation with the use of a lever. Here we are going to talk about how to Leverage our strengths, the people around us and tools in order to help us achieve our goals. Leverage can be defined as achieving maximum results with minimum effort that is when efficient ways of working are endorsed.

In order to leverage your strengths you must first know what they are. List down your strengths here. What can you do to leverage and increase these strengths:

_____

_____

_____

_____

Now think about your goals and the things you want to achieve – how can you leverage your strengths to achieve your goals? What strengths do you already possess which you can use to help you find your dream job, get a promotion, open a business or achieve what your goal is? List your answers to these questions down here.

_____

_____

_____

_____

_____

Think about your circle of friends and acquaintances, what people can help you achieve your goals? Maybe they already work in your field of interest; maybe they can help you out with a loan; maybe you could enter into a joint venture with them to expand your business? Who can you leverage to achieve the life of your dreams? List your answers to these questions down here:

_____

_____

_____

_____

_____

What tools can you leverage to become more productive, to automate your business, or to get more done in less time? List them here:

_____

_____

_____

_____

_____

LOVE

As the author Franklin once said "Love doesn't make the world go round. Love is what makes the ride worthwhile."

In order to have more love in your life you must first decide to accept and love yourself instead of beating yourself up about things or finding fault in the way you look or the things you do. Resolve to love yourself instead. Love and accept yourself right now. A technique I use when using Emotional Freedom Therapy on clients is to encourage them to love and accept themselves no matter what.

I remember a few years ago I attended a Brian Tracy seminar and was told to repeat the following affirmation ten times every single morning as soon as I wake up "I love myself, I love myself, I love myself". Resolve to say this to yourself today. Do it NOW.

Mother Teresa left a legacy of love and in her words said "It's not what you do, but how much love you put into it that matters".

A cup of love will replace any anger, fear, resentment, disappointments. Think of the things in your life right now where you attach negative feelings to. Write them down

_____

_____

_____

_____

_____

_____

_____

Now close your eyes, be still, relax, take deep breathes. Imagine a golden cup of love; make it as big as you can with each breath. Pour the golden love on the negative feeling. Feel its warmth and its glow. Notice how you feel – more relaxed, calm, peaceful, and happy. Open your eyes knowing that you only now have love.

Without love there is nothing. Love should be your top priority. Life is bankrupt without love. Every single relationship you have in your life should matter. I think you and I have been guilty of saying we will make time for people in our life as though we have to 'schedule' them in. I remember visiting a very special friend of mine in Australia. On my first morning in Australia I sat having a coffee over looking Sydney Harbour thinking to myself "It is only twenty four hours away, why did it take me so long to get here". When people are special, they count in your life. They are not a schedule; they are a natural extension of you.

List the people in your life that you need to spend time with or pay a special visit to now. Phone them and let them know you are on your way. _____What are the ways that you can bring more love into your life?

_____

_____

_____

_____

_____

_____

What do you think is the benefit of having more love in your life?

_____

_____

_____

_____

_____

_____

_____

LEGACY

This is your opportunity to start being and acting NOW in the way in which you would like to be remembered. In this exercise imagine three famous people or people that you know who have left a lasting legacy. Write them down here.

_____

_____

_____

_____

_____

Now list what is they are remembered for? What impact have they have on the world or their community?

_____

_____

_____

_____

_____

Now write your obituary using exactly the words in which you would truly like to be remembered for.

_____

_____

_____

_____

_____

So now sign and date the following commitment -

I_____honour my commitment to start living by my Obituary NOW.

Date_____ Sign_____

MINDSET

All masters develop a positive mind set. Make a list of all the books, seminars or talks you can attend this year to help you develop a more positive mindset.

1. _____

2. _____

3. _____

4. _____

5. _____

6. _____

Another way to do this is by constantly repeating positive affirmations to yourself, until they become a reality for you. You can also write down your affirmations 20 times daily on a piece of paper, or repeat them to yourself either out loud or silently. Make sure that your affirmations are positive, in the present tense, include your name, be specific and use the word now.

Here is an example: "I, Jacky now tap into my unlimited mind of creation and draw from it the right thoughts, plans and actions that lead to mastery".

Write your own affirmations following these guidelines.

_____

_____

_____

_____

_____

MODELLING

What we mean by the term modelling is that we decide what it is we want to master by modelling somebody who already has the skill we desire and is successful at that skill. Instead of an external factor that influences our behaviour (i.e. parents, peers); we ourselves choose to consciously copy or model the behaviour of others in order to achieve more in our lives. A pre-supposition of modelling is 'modelling successful performance leads to excellence'. You have a natural gift of learning and when you are shown how to use your mind and body productively your quality of performance will be increased. Model a successful person with the skill you desire and copy what they do until you get the same results. Clarify and define the behaviours and steps that you need to produce the results required. Identify what is essential for success.

List down some successful people whose traits/success/behaviours you greatly admire:

_____

_____

_____

_____

_____

List down the behaviours/qualities/habits that these people display which contribute to their greatness:

_____

_____

_____

_____

_____

How can you incorporate this same behaviour into your life to make you more successful, list your ideas down here.

_____

_____

_____

_____

_____

MAGNETIC

A magnetic personality is a person with natural charisma, self-confidence and incredible positive energy; these are people that you feel drawn to and want to be around, these are also people whose requests you do not mind fulfilling. When you and I have such a personality, we would find it far easier to achieve our goals and attain mastery as we would be able to influence people and achieve results in a faster and better manner.

This visualisation exercise will help -

Picture yourself as a magnet.

You magnetise positive energy.

Each vibration of your magnetic energy radiates a positive energy – empathy, consideration, warmth, gentleness, smiles, laughter, presence, joy, concern, engaging.

Positive experiences are all around you. You are so powerful.

People are drawn towards you they are powerless to resist your energy and charm. They naturally want to be in your presence.

Open your eyes and really BE that magnet today.

Make a decision to be more magnetic today. Spend time really putting into practice these techniques I have outlined below with everyone that you meet today.

Write out the impact that it had on your interactions here:

_____

_____

_____

_____

_____

1. Radiate empathy towards everyone that you come into contact with.

2. Follow our steps outlined earlier to become more self-confidence

3. Be present in the moment when interacting with someone

4. Maintain a positive mindset

5. Make sure you laugh and smile with people around you

6. Be engaging and engaged in conversation

7. Pay meaningful compliments to people

8. Be considerate and understanding with people around you

MEDITATION

Many masters will apply stillness and meditation. Meditation is not prayer, mediation is a deep awareness and is a state when your mind if free from all distractions and fleeting thoughts. Think of mediation as a tool to help still your mind in order to provide you with greater clarity and a sense of calm and peace. The stillness of mind and body practised on a regular basis will help you inhibit all thoughts so that worry and fear are dissolved and replaced with only desirable thoughts.

Here is a simple technique to learn how to meditate for beginners:

1. Make time to meditate, preferably early in the morning, remember to meditate at the same time every day.

2. Do not meditate when you are too full or too hungry as both prove to be distracting.

3. Find or create a relaxing and quiet environment

4. Sit on the ground, with your legs crossed and your back straight, you can also use a cushion if you want to.

5. Close your eyes and do not focus on anything

6. Breathe deeply and slowly from your abdomen rather than your chest. You should feel your stomach rise and fall while your chest stays relatively still.

7. Breath in through your nostrils and out through your mouth

8. Be perfectly still and inhibit all thought

9. Still the chatter in your head, you can even repeat a mantra like 'aum' to help you relax.

10. Relax all your muscles from your head to your feet so tension is eliminated and mentally let go of all anxieties

11. Make mental pictures of pleasant associations and see every detail

12. Use your imagination so that you create all that is perfect. Make your vision clear and complete.

13. Notice what you see, what is happening around you, the colours, the smells, the tastes? What are you feeling, what do you see? Who else is with you.

14. When you are ready slowly come back and open your eyes.

Write down the time that you will commit to meditating on a daily basis here: _____

Each week meditate on specific areas of your life and your goals using the techniques above. Write down what you need to meditate on specifically.

_____

_____

_____

_____

_____

Have there been times when you have experienced feelings of self-doubt and even low self-confidence? Developing an attitude of never giving up can actually help you overcome these feelings and face the challenges with a positive outlook and self-confidence.

To achieve mastery you need to develop a Never Give Up attitude. View any obstacles in your path as nothing but minor delays and temporary setbacks rather than a reason to throw in the towel.

Repeat the manta "never give up" to yourself every time the going gets hard, and remember to read the stories of people like you who have faced worse situations and adversaries and who overcame them and triumphed. These stories are an amazing source of inspiration and motivation when we are in doubt.

Place the words NEVER GIVE UP somewhere you can see them to remind you to keep faith alive. Write them and place them where you can see them right now.

What are the benefits to you to have a 'never give up' attitude in your life?

_____

_____

_____

What can you do each day to keep this attitude alive so that it becomes automatic?

_____

_____

_____

OPTIMISM

Remember we become what we think, so if you think you are an optimist you will become one. Life will be easier, more pleasant and full of opportunity for you. However if you think you are a pessimist, then you will become one and view yourself as a victim of your circumstances. Negative thinking will not produce good results. A happy optimistic mind will produce your best work.

You will have created Neuro pathways with your old habits and they have a craving so will be unwilling to accept change. When you create new habits new Neuro pathways are also created. This happens with practice and persistence. The opposite of optimism is pessimism. Your positive energy will need to be predominant and stronger than your negative energy in order to stop being pessimistic. Your goal should be to feel better, to be more optimistic. Resolve to become an optimist today and apply the 4 techniques listed here and see how they make you feel better.

Four ways to become more optimistic:

- Exercise or meditate to release stress and tension

- Always see the positive aspect of difficult situations

- Think positive thoughts

- Spend time away from negative people and enjoy the company of positive people instead, 'model' their behaviours.

What else can you do to feel good now? List 20 things that you can do to make you feel good now.

_____

_____

_____

ORIGINALITY

What makes you stand out from the crowd? In order for you to be original you must first be aware of who you are and what it is that makes you – you. List down at least twenty things that identifies who you are, the things that make you unique and special:

_____

_____

_____

_____

_____

Now circle six of these words that really identifies who you are and makes you stand out. Now write your identity statement.

For example when I did this my identity statement became: I am an outstanding, successful, compassionate, dynamic leader who inspires people to be the best they can be.

_____

_____

_____

_____

_____

Commit to one action every day to express your uniqueness and identity statement. List what you will do in the next seven days.

Example: you can express your compassion by raising funds for people in need.

_____

_____

_____

_____

_____

_____

OMNIPOTENT

When you are omnipotent you have the belief that you are capable of doing anything that you set out to achieve. If you believe that you are an omnipotent or all powerful being, then you will find no obstacles that are powerful enough to deter you from your goals and keep you from achieving mastery.

This belief is more a state of mind, and is also a self-fulfilling prophecy. The more you believe you are omnipotent, the harder you will strive to remove all obstacles from your path, the more you will achieve your goals, this will then validate your belief in your omnipotence and motivate you to achieve more.

To be omnipotent will mean time and time again you will need to step out of your comfort zone, remove those obstacles, and face those challenges. To operate within your comfort zone will not stretch you. A master with a winning, all encompassing desire will powerfully succeed in all they set out to do. To do so they constantly stretches themselves. Are you operating within your comfort zone? It very often is a natural tendency. When you stretch yourself and achieve, you expand and create another comfort zone and you will be able to be stretched again. Only when you stretch yourself will you realise your full potential and power.

Write down one of your goals here using the six P.s

_____

_____

_____

_____

_____

_____

Now strongly visualise yourself achieving it. What do you see, hear and feel? What is your state?

Were you in your stretch zone, comfort zone or maybe you were hesitating and panicking? If you were not in the stretch zone you will need to alter you goal. If you were hesitating, identify what the obstacle or fear is.

Write down any obstacles which you encountered and what you would need to put into place to overcome these?

_____

_____

_____

_____

_____

_____

_____

It you were in your comfort zone, how will you make the goal more challenging and stretching?

_____

_____

_____

_____

_____

_____

_____

PURPOSE

Living on purpose and in purpose is the realisation of every master. They are truly living their life with a purpose. Without a true purpose you may frequently change your job, career, relationships, and direction in life. Your life experiences including your hurt and disappointments will equip you for your life purpose. What lessons have you learnt from life experiences? Examine what you are good at and this will be a clue to your purpose. What talents lie dormant within you? What do you really enjoy doing?

List all your talents and abilities here:

_____

_____

_____

_____

Circle the ones which give you joy, passion, motivation, inspiration, pleasure, happiness, contentment and fulfilment. Now ask yourself – in what way do I see myself passionately serving others and loving it?

_____

_____

_____

_____

_____

Now state your ideal life purpose:

_____

_____

_____

_____

_____

What actions can you take towards living your ideal life purpose?

_____

_____

_____

_____

_____

PASSION

Passion coach Curt Rosengren defines passion "as the energy that comes from being more of YOU into what you do". It is the love that you have for a particular task or activity that energizes you and drives you to put more of yourself into that activity.

The first question you must answer is - what are you passionate about?

Example: I am passionate about helping people by inspiring them to live an empowered life.

_____

_____

_____

_____

_____

Now that you have identified what makes you passionate, what can you do that excites you and energizes you and keeps that passion alive for you every single day.

Example: I coach at least 5 clients a week, every single week

_____

_____

_____

_____

_____

What can you to sustain and have continuous passion in your life now and on going? Write down some ways now.

Example: By creating programs like 'Aspiring to Mastery', I am able to reach out to and help thousands of people around the world.

_____

_____

_____

_____

POTENTIAL

Each person on this planet has the potential for greatness and mastery; however fear is what often stops us from rising up and achieving our potential. Fear is False Evidence Appearing Real. Usually there is no evidence to support the fear. When you project into the future you create a situation which has not yet arisen, so why place fear into your future? Fear sometimes also has a history. This may be fear of failure, fear of success, fear of lack. Confronting your fears, taking action and doing something will often dissolve your fear.

Your vocabulary can direct your fear into power. For instance -

FEAR	POWER
I should	I could
It is a problem	It is an opportunity
This has not worked out	I am learning and growing
Life is a struggle	life offers opportunities
I hope	I know
I do not know	I will find a solution
Its not my fault	I am fully responsible
I have failed	I have learnt a valuable lesson
I can not do this	I can find a way to do this
The task is too huge for me	I can complete the task by breaking it down into manageable chunks

What fears, insecurities and doubts do you have, which are preventing you from achieving your potential?

_____

_____

_____

_____

_____

_____

Resolve now to let go of these insecurities and doubts about yourself. Change your vocabulary. Formulate positive affirmations to help you let go of these insecurities and doubts and write them down here.

_____

_____

_____

_____

_____

_____

PHILANTHROPIC

Many people who have achieved greatness are also great philanthropists; they understand another law of the universe, which is the more you give of yourself in terms of time and money, the more the universe will give back to you.

Here are some ways to practice philanthropy in your life:

1. Give some of your time to charity and non-profit organisations

2. Visit an elderly person to keep them company

3. Donate a percentage of your yearly income

4. Volunteer your skills, for example: if you are a lawyer you can offer to do some free legal work for your favourite non-profit organisation.

5. Have a yard/garage/bake sale and donate the profits to your favourite charity.

6. Enlist the help of your friends and neighbours to raise money for the charity you want to support and give together.

What are the two things you are going to do this week to be more philanthropic? Write them down here.

_____

_____

_____

_____

_____

_____

_____

_____

QUALITATIVE

There may have been times when how much you could do or produce took precedence over how well you did something or the quality of the product. However to achieve mastery we are more concerned with the quality of our output before going onto producing the quantity.

Make a habit of developing a quality conscious today:

1. At work spend more time on a project, spend time on research and going through it a few times before you hand it in.

2. With family and friends, focus on spending quality time with them, make the time you spend together meaningful and memorable.

3. Go through your home, what items can you replace with 'quality' items, get rid of the clutter or the 'quantity'. Practice this with your wardrobe as well.

4. Be mindful of quality when you are watching TV, reading books and magazines and listening to music.

5. When shopping for groceries, buy the freshest and best quality ingredients you can afford. You will be surprised at how much better food tastes when you start with better quality ingredients.

6. Choose your friends and peers with the same care that you choose expensive clothes – pick quality over quantity.

What ways will you incorporate quality in your life in order to achieve mastery?

_____

_____

QUICK WITTED

Learning to be quick witted is simply a matter of expanding your knowledge, learning to think faster and more clearly and also being able to focus on the situation and understand it better to enable you to rationalize, evaluate and make quick and better decisions.

Here are some strategies on how to become quicker witted:

Read more

Be observant about human nature

Spend some time each day doing mental exercises

Attend a creativity or imagination workshop

Be aware of your surroundings

Be humorous however not sarcastic or caustic

Allow yourself to be impulsive

Trust your instinct , apply rational and evaluation

What two strategies are you going to apply to your life today to enable you to become quick witted? List them down here.

RESPONSIBILITY

Responsibility is the realisation that you are 100% responsible for your life and where you are in life right now. You and you alone are responsible for your thoughts, actions and reactions to all circumstances that have arisen in your life. When things go wrong ask: why did this happen; what did I do to contribute to this; what could I have done differently? Being responsible is taking complete control for everything that happens in your life which will enable you to make rationalised and better decisions.

Being responsible can mean:

1. Accept now that you and only you are responsible for the choices that you make in your life.

2. Accepting that you are responsible for what YOU CHOOSE to feel and think

3. Accepting that you chose the direction that your life will take

4. Accepting that you cannot blame others for your choices and bad decisions or circumstances

5. Accepting that how you feel about something is entirely up to you.

6. Taking responsibility for your health and well-being

7. Taking ownership of being your own cheerleader, writing your own affirmations and forming your own motivating thoughts.

Think of times in your life when you have not had the outcome you would have liked to have had. Who did you blame; what did you blame? What would have happened if you had taken responsibility?

_____

_____

_____

_____

_____

Write down the aspects of your life that you now commit to taking responsibility for: _____

_____

_____

_____

_____

The next time you are feeling negative or find yourself not taking responsibility for your actions, here are some things you can do:

1. Remember the law of cause and effect; realize that everything you do in your life will have a consequence, think of this consequence before you take action.

2. Do not look for ways to assign blame, look for solutions instead. Instead of focusing on whose fault it was, focus instead of how you can fix it.

3. Forgive yourself for any shortcomings you have.

4. Think positive thoughts and shun bad ones – use your affirmations to help you maintain a healthy, positive mindset.

RIGOUR

Rigour simply means to do something consistently over a period of time in order to achieve results.

The power of rigour is that it is a consistent and focussed effort throughout the entire duration of a project and not just in the beginning and the end.

In order to maintain rigour, you need first have a plan in place for completing a task or a project. Write this plan down and paste it where you can see it. Do something every single day to bring you closer to completing your goal. Recognize that most of us are motivated towards the beginning and the end of the project, so build in rewards for the middle. Every time you complete one step or section of the project, spend time celebrating your success and rewarding yourself.

What project you are working on right now? Write down a project plan for this now, make sure you put in time lines and milestones along with the rewards that you will give yourself for achieving each milestone. Resolve to stick to this plan no matter what.

_____

_____

_____

_____

_____

_____

_____

_____

REASON

We know that motivation can be both external and internal and that internal motivation is often stronger and more powerful than external motivation. One of the ways to effectively motivate yourself to do something from within is to identify the reason that you are doing it in the first place.

Write down your reasons for wanting to achieve your goals here, go back to these reasons every time you become derailed or feel a little unmotivated to achieve your targets.

Example: My reason for writing this program is to help as many people as possible achieve mastery and to be a best-selling self-help author.

_____

_____

_____

_____

_____

_____

_____

SOLUTIONS

The next time you face a problem or a difficult situation, you need to consciously tell yourself to STOP focussing on the problem and start focussing on finding a solution instead. There is without doubt always a solution to every single problem however complex or simple it may appear to be. The problem that you cannot solve does not exist.

To find a solution to a problem ask questions that begin with WHAT or HOW, don't ask questions that begin with WHY, WHEN or WHO.

Also focus on what 'you' can do versus what people outside your sphere of control can do. Ensure that your solution is action – oriented and take action as soon as you can.

Write down a problem you are facing here:

_____

_____

_____

_____

_____

_____

_____

_____

Now focus on finding the solutions for the problem:

_____

_____

_____

_____

_____

_____

_____

_____

STRATEGY

A strategy is always going to be a sequence of thoughts in which you use in order to think and plan your actions to achieve your outcomes. Strategies are the key ways in which we either do or do not achieve our desired outcome. Our internal processing strategies control our external behaviours. It is important that the desired outcome has a defined sensory representation. You need to have belief that the outcome is worth doing, you can do it, and you deserve to do it. All strategies that are successful will use specific language and words that will stimulate the senses – the vision, the feeling, the sound, the taste, the smell. A strategy is essentially a plan with clear cut objectives that you want to achieve, and goals that you wish to accomplish.

Once you have a strategy, how do you know it is the best strategy? Running through it several times and examining it to see if anything needs changing is one way of changing a strategy.

The other way is to use the TOTE model from NLP to evaluate if your strategy is working or not.

TOTE stands for:

Test – the strategy that you want to implement. What do you want to achieve. What outcome do you want? What is your present state? What is your desired state?

Operate – do the actions that make up the strategy. What can you do to reduce the present state and increase the desired state?

Test – see if the actions have the desired effect. To what extent have you reduced the difference between the present state and the desired state?

Exit – has the outcome been achieved? Is there no difference between the present state and the desired state? Exit the strategy if this is the case, or develop a new one if the outcome has not been achieved.

What three goals or projects in your life that you have right now do you need a strategy for? Commit to using the TOTE model for them. Notice the following as you use this model -

What do you do to get your outcome?

What specifically are the steps and stages that you go through?

When you are not succeeding, what other choices can you make?

What do you do to overcome unexpected difficulties?

_____

_____

_____

_____

_____

_____

_____

_____

_____

_____

_____

_____

_____

_____

SYSTEMS

Systems are processes that exist to ensure that work is carried out in a prescribed manner.

In systems we also need to look at those systems which become efficient repeatable actions in order for us to fulfil our goals in the most effective way possible. This may be automation, service standards, performance, evaluation and time keeping.

Evaluate what systems you need in place –

What is not happening at the moment that needs to happen?

What outcomes do you want?

What gaps are there?

What efficiencies need to be built in?

Who needs to be involved?

Make a list of the systems you can incorporate in your life today in order to become more efficient.

_____

_____

_____

_____

_____

_____

_____

SPIRIT

To be infused with spirit is to live with vitality and energy, enthusiasm and confidence which you share with others. It is often referred to as the spirit into which we enter into something. It is this spirit which we must strive for continuously. Living with true spirit will raise your level of consciousness in all areas of your life so that you are living in a spirit and consciousness of more happiness, health, wealth, power. When you live within the spirit of such things, they will naturally be a part of you and yours by a right. When we recognise our spiritual nature our accomplishments increase as enthusiasm, desire, courage and faith are developed further. Being a person of Spirit, can help us face each day with more energy and enthusiasm and make our personal and work relationships stronger and more meaningful.

Resolve to be a person who lives with spirit today. Note down the ways in which you will live in a spirit of higher consciousness.

Examples I use are- I always have a clear focused vision and everything works perfectly in my life.

There are many opportunities for me to learn from.

_____

_____

_____

_____

_____

_____

_____

STRENGTH

The path to mastery and achieving our goals is one of great labour and we will face many obstacles and setbacks along the way. Any thoughts of lack, limitation, fear, or distress will produce exactly that. The way to overcome these disappointments and setbacks is to develop your inner strength which allows you to remain strong, focussed and positive despite all adversity. Out of effort emerges strength. Develop a permanent inner strength.

Many things people fear do not actually happen. Worry has never solved anything. Rationalise your fears and limitations. Look at the probabilities of them happening. Ask yourself, what is the worst thing that can possibly happen, and what can I do to prevent it happening? So what if it happens? Each time you exert some staying power and face your challenges head on, your positive self image will grow as will your inner strength.

List the challenges and fears you have in your life right now. Rationalise them and state what action you can take to overcome them.

_____

_____

_____

_____

_____

_____

_____

_____

SERVICE

To be really very serious about attracting wealth and success into your life you will need to focus on an idea of how you can be of Service to others. Spend some time reflecting on your answers to these questions.

How can you help people? _____

How can you be of a service to them? _____

How can you give greater value? _____

How can you help them to make money? _____

If you are employed, think of more ways that you can be of a service to your employer in order that they reward you with remuneration and promotion. _____

How can you help and be of service to your peers, customers, your boss, stakeholders, and systems? _____

_____

_____

_____

How can you be of service to everybody that you come into contact with?

_____

_____

_____

_____

_____

Your very intentions will be based upon some core principles and laws of fairness and integrity in order for this to work. Find out what people need, how you can be of service to them and supply this service to them with fairness and integrity.

TENACITY

Tenacity is the courage and persistence to repeat something over and over again, and to stick to a routine or schedule in order to achieve mastery. Develop habits around the things that really matter and do them as though they really matter.

What goal really matters to you and no matter what you must complete it?

_____

_____

_____

_____

_____

What habits can you develop in order to be tenacious and what routines or schedules do you think will help you achieve mastery in your life?

_____

_____

_____

_____

_____

_____

In order to be more tenacious you need to commit completely to what you want to achieve. Write down your commitment to being more tenacious in your goal achievement.

_____

_____

_____

_____

_____

_____

Why should we be more tenacious? Think back on your life and reflect on the answer to these questions.

What are the situations in your life when you wish you had given it one more attempt, or experimented a little harder in order to achieve something you really wanted? Did you ever quit before you got what you wanted and wished you hadn't? What was that situation and how do you feel about it? Write down your thoughts here.

_____

_____

_____

_____

_____

_____

What would be the rewards in your life if you applied more tenacity to your goals?

_____

_____

_____

_____

_____

_____

_____

THOUGHT

Thought is most powerful. A thought is a physical thing that goes out to the universe. You get what you think about most of the time. Whether or not you are consciously aware of the Law of Attraction it is working for you. That explains why people who are successful are using the Law of Attraction whether they know about it or not. You will become aware of why you DO NOT have or DO have what you want in your life when you realise how the Law of Attraction works and start to consciously apply it. As was taught in the movie the Secret, thoughts become things. Yes, we really do become what we think we are.

Look at your BE, DO, HAVE list. What positive thoughts do you need to have to create the life of your dreams? List them here.

_____

_____

_____

_____

What positive affirmations do you commit to repeating to yourself over and over again in order to BE DO HAVE?

_____

_____

_____

_____

_____

_____

What effect do you envision these affirmations and positive thoughts having on your life and the achievement of all that you want in your life?

_____

_____

_____

_____

_____

_____

Be careful of how to ask for things! For instance if you state that by the end of next year you want to live in the house of your dreams, and then you say how will I afford the up keep of it, the Universe may well have been making preparations to deliver your dream home and then became confused by your added thoughts which are your counter intentions, and thinks that you do not really want your dream home.

What positive added thoughts can you use to support your main goal?

_____

_____

_____

_____

_____

_____

TRUTH

It is important that you to commit to speaking the truth as much as possible in your interaction with yourself and with others. Truth is the very foundation of every relationship.

Commit to speaking the truth always in these three situations:

We must tell the truth when people have the right to know the truth such as when selling someone a new service or product.

Second, we must tell the truth with the relationships we are in be it our spouse, business partner, clients customers etc.

Thirdly – we must tell the truth to people if their well-being depends on that truth.

What do you think is the value of telling the truth as much as possible? What impact will this have on your life and on your interactions with others?

_____

_____

_____

UNIVERSAL MIND

Remember from our discussion earlier the Universal Mind is the common bond or thread that connects all living things across the world. This bond or common consciousness is what we call the universal mind and it is something that connects each and every one of us. By tapping into this consciousness we can achieve the things we want in life and find the answers to all our questions. This starts with your conscious mind. Everything in your conscious mind must be positive as already mentioned as this is transferred to your sub conscious mind which then connects to the universal mind. Your thoughts become your reality.

One of the ways to tap into the universal mind is through meditation; we have already talked about the power of meditation and how to meditate earlier in the program. Follow the guidelines for meditation.

Use this step by step process to tap into the universal mind:

- Commit to maintaining an open mind; tell yourself your outer world is in fact created by your inner world.

- Ask for exactly what you do want. Be very specific and clear.

- Use positive affirmations to focus your thoughts. On a separate piece of paper, write down all your affirmations you want to say to yourself every single day. Start saying these affirmations right now.

- Give every day: your time, your energy, your kind words, and your money. It will ultimately make its way back to you.

- Meditate twice a day to increase your ability to tap into this source. When you meditate focus on your vision and on the things you want.

- Have faith and belief always that the things you want or believe in will come to you.

UNSTOPPABLE

We must believe in our own ability to be UNSTOPPABLE! Throughout history the one common thread that runs through people who we consider unstoppable is their passion for their goal and their determination to achieve their goals despite all odds.

Why are you passionate about your goals? Why do you feel your goals are important?

_____

_____

_____

_____

_____

How do you commit to following through on your goals and dreams until you become unstoppable despite the obstacles and the challenges you face.

_____

_____

_____

_____

_____

VALUES

As already discussed in this program, the times when goals are not achieved are usually when they are not in alignment with your values. In order to achieve the things you want, you must first understand your values and then evaluate whether your goals are in alignment with these values. Values are what are essential to you, the things that really matter, and the things you truly stand for. When you are clear about your values they will make an impact on every decision that you make which in turn will determine your destiny.

For instance, some of my top values are integrity, love, honesty, passion, compassion, joy.

Identify your ten top values and write them down. Then place your values in a hierarchy, the most important value being at the top.

_____

_____

_____

_____

_____

_____

_____

In what order do your values need to be in order to fulfill your ultimate destiny and what benefit do they bring to you?

_____

_____

_____

_____

_____

_____

Are there any values you could eliminate in order to fulfill your ultimate destiny and if so why?

_____

_____

_____

_____

_____

_____

Now look at each value and write the answers to these questions;-What are the rules you attach to each value? In other words what has to happen in order for that value to be fulfilled? Do these rules empower or disempower? What rules can you eliminate in order to fulfill your ultimate destiny?

Now look at your list of goals which you have already written. Do your goals match your values? What changes do you need to make so that your goals are congruent to your values?

_____

_____

_____

_____

_____

_____

VISION

Remember, a vision is a powerful force that will change and direct your life. A personal vision statement will influence your choices and help guide you in your decisions on a daily basis. Your vision statement is a picture of how you want your life to be encompassing your life goals, values, beliefs and passion while demonstrating your success and achievement.

Throughout this workbook on Aspiring to Mastery we have worked on all of the elements of your vision statement – your goals, your belief, your values, your passion and much more. Go back to these exercises and write every word here that you wrote in those exercises. Circle the ones that portray your vision and from these very special words write your very own vision statement. Write it bold.

My example when I did this exercise is this: I Jacqueline am a committed, successful, compassionate, awesome leader who impacts peoples life's inspiring them to achieve mastery.

_____

_____

_____

_____

_____

_____

_____

_____

_____

Now create your vision board. Go back to your BE, DO, HAVE list and your goals. Gather magazines and cut out pictures and words to create everything from these lists on your vision board. If there is anything you have not included, include it NOW. If there is anything you want to change - change it NOW. Create ALL that you want to BE, DO and HAVE in your life. Take as long as you want to with this. This is your manifestation.

When your vision board is complete, take it to your place of meditation and follow the meditation exercise with your vision board. In your meditation place yourself in your vision. Notice what you are feeling, seeing, saying to yourself. Just how amazing is your life now?

VIBRATION

Remember to attract something into your life, raise your vibration to match that of the person or object that you desire. You will be attracted to things and other people who are of the same frequency of vibration. Positive vibrations such as love, peace, balance, harmony, joy within you will raise your vibration. Everything is energy that vibrates at a different frequency.

Exercise: The Vibrational Steps.

This is an exercise I use with my clients when their vibrational energies need to be lifted especially when they are in a low emotional state.

Think of a time when you have experienced a low emotional state. At each stage it is good to acknowledge the vibrational state that you are in. Recognise it and identity the source of it for when you have given it full acknowledgement you will be able to progress on to the next increased vibrational level a step at a time.

The Vibrational steps -

Step one – low self esteem, depression, fear.

Step two - resentment, anger, hurt.

Step three – discouraged, overwhelmed.

Step four - impatient, frustrated, pessimistic.

Step five - hopefulness, clarity.

Step six - acceptance, contentment.

Step seven - optimistic, eager, positive expectation.

Step eight - happy, free, happy, joyful, empowered.

When you have acknowledged each emotional step that you are on, see the next step in front of you and step onto it, feel and acknowledge the emotions and let go. Ask yourself what has changed? What do you feel now? Let your inner guidance reveal and uncover the next emotional vibration. Each time step onto the next step which will increase your vibrational intensity until you eventually reach step eight of the feelings of being free, joy, happy, empowered.

In your step eight in a state of freedom, joy, happyness, empowerment - state your positive expectations and live in emotional alignment.

Here are some things that I do to make myself feel better and lift my vibration.

- Listen to an upbeat song

- Watch comedy shows

- Watch a funny movie

- Write in a gratitude journal

- Go for a walk in nature

- Exercise

- Do something nice for someone

- Play with a pet

- Clean and de-clutter

- Read or listen to something motivational

List the ways in which you can increase your level of vibration and do one of them straight away. Notice how you feel.

_____

_____

_____

_____

_____

_____

VITALITY

Vitality in essence means energy. When you are full of energy and vitality the more you are able to achieve your goals and achieve mastery. Self esteem, well being and energy increases.

To increase vitality levels you can commit to the following -

1. Increase your oxygen levels by deeply breathing oxygen into your lungs.

2. Meditate.

3. Drink plenty of water.

4. Carry out body stretching exercises such as yoga or Pilates.

5. Walk regularly.

6. Take up a form of aerobic exercise.

7. Detox your body

8. Reduce your consumption of acids, dairy products, animal flesh, fats and oils

9. Eat water rich foods such as fruit, salad and vegetables.

10. Take time to eat and digest your food. Be relaxed at meal times.

11. Eat natural, nourishing and organic foods.

12. De-stress your mind and keep positive constructive thoughts

What foods can you eat that will make you feel more energetic and full of vitality?

_____

_____

_____

_____

_____

_____

_____

_____

Write down and commit to five things that will increase your energy and vitality. On a scale of one to ten how full of vitality do you commit to being? How will you achieve this level of vitality?

_____

_____

_____

_____

_____

_____

_____

_____

_____

_____

_____

WILL

As already discussed in the program, belief is what fuels your actions. Will is your inner strength for self mastery and decisiveness. Will is your inner ability to overcome excuses, laziness, and procrastination. Will is your innate ability to make a decision and stick with it despite how difficult it seems. A true master will - will himself to succeed despite setbacks and adversity. They have a desire so strong that they have ultimate persistence in their goal achievement. Without persistence and willpower, desire for the goal accomplishment will diminish.

Think of the times when you have lacked willpower. Was the reasons lack of desire, fear of criticism, lack of focus, lack of ambition, no clarity, no purpose, no planning? These are some reasons and you may have others. Write your reasons here and what it has cost you.

_____

_____

_____

_____

_____

_____

Some ways to increase willpower are -

1. Clarity of purpose. 2. Well formed plans. 3. A meaningful goal. 4. A strong desire. 5. Research and knowledge that is accurate. 6. Belief.

Now list the ways in which you will increase your willpower. Make this personal to you so that you are able to rely upon it when you need form good willpower habits in the future.

_____

_____

_____

_____

_____

_____

WISDOM

Wisdom is a trait that is much envied and is present in people from across all age groups. This is a trait you have and may not have developed it. It is still possible to cultivate it in your life. Wisdom is to have the true meaning and understanding of things to enable you to humbly reason and make wise choices and decisions.

To develop your wisdom you can do the following:

1. Learn to trust your instincts. Listen to the voice inside you. This is your intuition, your guidance and intuition from within.

2. Ask yourself wisdom accessing questions that start with what and how.

3. Track in a notebook the times when you relied on your instinct and record the results that followed.

4. Make a habit of reading every day to increase your knowledge and education.

5. Refrain from jumping to conclusions.

6. Consider reasons, causes, intent and outcomes before making a decision – think things through.

What do you need to do to cultivate your wisdom?

_____

_____

_____

_____

_____

WEALTH

Remember that wealth is a feeling of abundance and means different things to different people. How abundant on a scale of 1-10 do you consider yourself in the various aspects of your life. Tick all that apply.

Personal

Professional

Spiritual

Environmental

Financial

Now let's look at some steps to wealth.

1. Step 1 – changing the way we thing about money: use affirmations such as "I am wealthy and abundant" or "prosperity will be drawn to me from many places".

2. Step 2 – Understanding the power of small amounts. Start depositing something into your bank account every month. As you start accumulating wealth, your desire to accumulate it will also grow.

3. Step 3 – Savings = Freedom. Start thinking about savings as a means to freedom from the current restrictions you face.

4. Step 4 – Your financial fortress is your responsibility. Take responsibility for building your finances today and in the future in the way of savings, investments and insurance.

5. Step 5 – buy the stock not the product. Smart wealthy people know that when they like a product or love what it does for

them, they seek advise often placing their money in the stock not in the product.

6. Step 6 – invest in yourself first by saving 10% of your income. Before you pay your bills, pay yourself. Put money in your savings account first not last.

7. Step 7 – Stop worrying about money, you will only attract more of the situations you are worrying about. Remember the law of attraction does not know the difference between what you want and what you don't want, it only understands what you are focussing on.

8. Step 8 – how can you benefit others? The wealthiest people in history are people who created wealth for other people, how can you create wealth for other people and as a by product for yourself.

Everybody should have a major goal for financial freedom so they do not have to worry about money again. Do you know what that figure is for you.

As a guide the figure could be your mortgage and loans paid off, then multiply the income you need to live comfortably on each year by 20. What is your figure for you?

_____

_____

_____

_____

_____

_____

_____

Realise that wealth is within you. Wealth is thought as all wealth starts with an idea. Using your passion and purpose in life, what ideas do you have in which you can be of service to others.

_____

_____

_____

_____

_____

What added value can you put in to increase the wealth you get out?

_____

_____

_____

_____

_____

X FACTOR

I think you will agree that each and every one of us is unique and have qualities which are just as unique.

Think of three people you know that have the X factor. They can be famous people or someone you know and admire. What makes them stand out from the crowd?

_____

_____

_____

I think you will agree that these people accept their difference. They have unconditional acceptance, self confidence and self love.

What is your X-factor? What are the things that make you stand out from the crowd? You may know the answer to this already. To help you, ask three people for three words each that makes you different and stand out. Then write down what your X factor is.

_____

_____

_____

_____

_____

How can you celebrate your uniqueness and develop this in order to make it your X factor? _____

_____

_____

_____

Remember that channelling your X factor is also about being more confident and about being proud of the person that you are inside, commit to letting more of yourself shine through each day.

YEN

Remember that Yen means to have strong desire, or a strong unquenchable burning desire to achieve the things you want in life. In order to have a strong burning desire you need to be able to visualize your goals in great detail so you feel you already possess them.

Think of a time when you had a desire so strong and powerful to achieve your goal and not achieving it was not an option for you.

What became your driving force?

_____

_____

_____

_____

_____

What was your vision and how emotionally connected were you to your vision?

_____

_____

_____

_____

_____

What qualities and resources did you have that you could use again?

_____

_____

_____

_____

_____

What else could you do?

_____

_____

_____

_____

_____

_____

What would you do differently?

_____

_____

_____

_____

_____

What keeps you motivated and on track?

_____

_____

_____

_____

_____

ZEN

Zen as mentioned in the program is not only about meditation, it is also about the way we live and work. It is our entire approach to life and our environment.

Zen is about taking the time to meditate and rely on your intuition to help you make decisions. We have already spoken about meditation and relying on your intuition to help you make decisions.

One more aspect to incorporate in your life is the habit of maintaining a clean; clutter free and well organized workspace. Commit to cleaning your home and office today. One way to do this is to designate one room or area of your home to clean or organize every day of the week. Decide which area you will clean and organize on which day now.

- Monday:

- Tuesday:

- Wednesday:

- Thursday:

- Friday:

- Saturday:

- Sunday:

ZEST

So living with Zest makes you feel alive and full of life, it makes you feel free, joyful and uninhibited; it's what separates the mundane moments in life from the truly spectacular. Living with zest will increase your vibration. Commit to raising your intensity of vibration. Be outstanding in all that you do every day as you live in abundance with Zest.

Be on the top step of the vibrational steps! What does this mean to you? List every positive vibration in your body?

_____

_____

_____

_____

_____

_____

While you are in this state create your Breakthrough Goal. This can be in any area of your life. What one goal are you certain would have a huge massive impact in your life? Achieving it would be your ultimate success. What would you do if there were no limitations? What would you do if money were not an issue? What would you do if you knew you would not fail? What would you do if you had no fear? Visualise it using all your five senses. Be emotionally attached to it.

Write your Breakthrough Goal here.

_____

_____

_____

_____

_____

_____

_____

_____

How would achieving this change your life? What would you experience and are not experiencing now? Write everything you can think of.

_____

_____

_____

_____

_____

_____

_____

ZEAL

Being full of Zeal is like having a fire lit under you, which makes you want to achieve your goals. It makes you full of eagerness and enthusiasm. You are eager to serve your faith and belief with great passion and energy.

Together we have covered 62 fundamental foundation life principles to enable YOU to Aspire to Mastery. You truly are full of Zeal. You are an amazing unlimited being.

It is time to CELEBRATE as though you have achieved ALL OF YOUR DREAMS ASPIRATIONS AND GOALS. Step inside your dream now. Live your dreams now. What are you doing, what are you saying to yourself, what are other people saying to you, what house are you living in, what car do you drive, who is with you in your dream, what do you see, what purpose are you living with, what aromas are around you, what food do you taste, how much more have you learnt, how much love, joy, confidence passion and harmony do you have, how are you serving others, what ideas did you come up with, what are your thoughts, what colours are in your dream, what is your X Factor, how high is your vibration just how WEALTHY are you!

Celebrate all that you have achieved and say as many times as you like

THANK YOU, THANK YOU, THANK YOU

FOR ALL THAT I ASKED FOR,

FOR ALL THAT I BELIEVED IN,

FOR ALL THAT I RECEIVED.

YOUR MASTERY JOURNAL

Masters will always review what they have learnt and will constantly review their performance. There has been so much learning and personal growth in this program Aspiring To Mastery. You have covered so many aspects of mastery in an amazing journey. It is now time to review and journalise those learnings.

List the top life principles which made a big impact upon you which will now make the biggest contribution to your goals? List these in order of importance. State what difference these will make when these are implemented into your life on a daily basis.

_____

_____

_____

_____

_____

_____

_____

_____

_____

_____

_____

_____

State what the impact will be and what it will mean to you to implement all of these life principles into your life on a daily basis.

_____

_____

_____

_____

_____

_____

_____

_____

_____

_____

_____

_____

_____

_____

_____

_____

_____

_____

_____

_____

_____

What were your biggest challenges throughout the program? What did you learn about yourself as a result of these challenges?

_____

_____

_____

_____

_____

_____

_____

_____

_____

_____

_____

_____

_____

_____

_____

_____

_____

_____

_____

What 'light-bulb' moments did you have throughout the program? What did you learn from these and what difference will they make to your goal achievement?

_____

_____

_____

_____

_____

_____

_____

_____

_____

_____

_____

_____

_____

_____

_____

_____

_____

What inspirations did you gain and what will you do as a result of these inspirations?

_____

_____

_____

_____

_____

_____

_____

_____

_____

_____

_____

_____

_____

_____

_____

_____

_____

_____

What breakthroughs did you have and what difference will these make to your future?

_____

_____

_____

_____

_____

_____

_____

_____

_____

_____

_____

_____

_____

_____

_____

_____

_____

_____

What were your greatest successes and what will you do to increase your successes to accomplish your goals?

_____

_____

_____

_____

_____

_____

_____

_____

_____

_____

_____

_____

_____

_____

_____

_____

_____

_____

What other insights have you gained from Aspiring To Mastery.

_____

_____

_____

_____

_____

_____

_____

_____

_____

_____

_____

_____

_____

_____

_____

_____

_____

TO MY VERY VALUED READER AND AUDIENCE

Thank you for sharing this wonderful journey Aspiring To Mastery the Foundation. I know that you will see why I am so passionate about sharing these important life principles with you. I know that they will serve you well in your life as you practise and use them every day. There will be some wonderful changes in your life as magic and miracles are all around you. My wish for you is that you now lead a truly fullfilling, happy, inspired, empowered, transformed life; one in which you are following your true bliss with passion and joy as you live on purpose and with purpose being of service to others. I wish one day that we will meet and I welcome you to my workshop Aspiring To Mastery the Advancement where I will lead and demonstrate to you how to construct each and every principle so you can truly take these skills to another level. I welcome you to join and register at

www.AspiringTo Mastery.com.

With my warmest and fondest wishes

Jacqueline Day.

CPSIA information can be obtained
at www.ICGtesting.com
Printed in the USA
LVHW01s0018021018
592105LV00003B/868/P